I0117175

Mirror Training

Mirror Training

A Coach's Guide to Fostering Reflection and Growth in Male Athletes

Kip Ioane

©2024 All Rights Reserved. No portion of this book may be reproduced, stored in a retrieval system, or transmitted in any form or by any means-electronic, mechanical, photocopy, recording, scanning, or other-except for brief quotations in critical reviews or articles without the prior permission of the author.

Published by Game Changer Publishing

Paperback ISBN: 978-1-963793-72-7
Hardcover ISBN: 978-1-963793-73-4
Digital: ISBN: 978-1-963793-74-1

GC GAME CHANGER PUBLISHING

www.GameChangerPublishing.com

DEDICATION

For the soul of our profession.
For the future husbands, fathers, brothers, sons, and friends we inspire.
For the vision I've chased that I could no longer selfishly keep to myself.

Read This First

Just to say thank you for buying and reading my book, I would like to give you a few free bonus gifts, no strings attached!

To Download Your Free Gifts, Scan the QR Code:

#MirrorTraining

Mirror Training

A Coach's Guide to Fostering Reflection
and Growth in Male Athletes

Kip Ioane

GC GAME CHANGER
PUBLISHING

www.GameChangerPublishing.com

Table of Contents

Introduction

"Kip, what the hell is going on in Salem?"

Versions of that question, whether in face-to-face conversation, phone calls, text messages, or emails, came at me non-stop from friends, the parents of players, university alumni, and concerned community members. That cacophony marked a seismic shift in my approach to being an NCAA Division III men's basketball head coach and was the genesis point for everything that would become this book you are reading.

My name is Kip Ioane ("eye-own"). I have spent the last 25 years of my life in men's college basketball, four as a captain and player, seven as an assistant coach, and 14 and a half as a head college coach (note: while serving as an assistant coach at the college level, I was also a full-time high school teacher).

The self-reflection that resulted from this onslaught of phone calls, texts, and emails forced me into many long, sleepless nights. It opened my eyes to the fact that I was not doing what I had set out to do in the coaching profession. I was not committing time to building men capable of being quality husbands, fathers, sons, and members of society through basketball, which I consider to be the greatest game on the planet.

I decided then to recraft my philosophy and approach to coaching. That decision became the birth of #TeamsOfMen, LLC and the TeamsOfMen Coaching Framework. Now I work with athletes, coaches, and administrators from middle schools to Power Five universities as a speaker, workshop conductor, discussion and lesson plan creator, and curriculum assessor, helping them reimagine manhood and build positive masculinity every day.

Trigger Warning: Before I go any further, I want to note that this book contains discussions and descriptions of sensitive topics, including sexual assault, rape, and domestic violence. These references may be distressing or triggering for some readers. Reader discretion is advised. If you find yourself needing support, please consider reaching out to a mental health professional or a support group. Your wellbeing is important.

The incident that led to my awakening, the "asteroid crashing into earth," happened three years into my head coaching career, in the spring of 2013, at Willamette University in Salem, Oregon, when a high-profile sexual assault occurred on campus. At the same time, a local domestic violence case was making the rounds in the newspaper and social media. Finally, campus authorities unearthed the misogynistic Facebook group of a campus fraternity, rife with sexist, homophobic, and misogynistic remarks targeting female athletes and administrators.

All I could say when asked about this rash of incidents was, "Well, it's not my guys… My players didn't commit these acts." While that was technically true, I knew I had done nothing different (no training, no discussions, no education) for my men that could have contributed to them NOT making decisions like these. I hadn't done anything differently than coaches whose players were committing these acts. I couldn't claim to be better. And I couldn't sleep.

I couldn't sit with that because it wasn't who I was raised to be or who I wanted to be. I'd spent 38 of the 44 years of my life engrossed in athletics, evaluating my existence based on the status and exploits of my teams. My dad was an All-American college basketball player, a Hall of Fame high school and college coach, and a renowned high school teacher, and my mom was a 30-year administrator of a Montessori school.

Suffice it to say, my brother, Kane, and I were raised on the belief that athletics provided a sort of life education, that a coach was required to be more than an X's-and-O's tactician, that they should serve as trusted mentors and creators of second families for their players. I can remember countless dinners at our home with my dad's players and students. We got to know so many high school and college athletes and students because our parents were not only willing to provide a warm meal for them but also to model and expose them to the warmth and love of our family. Kane and I have spent our professional lives in the family business—me as a basketball coach and Kane as a college football coach.

But at this moment, I was failing at the example our parents had set… I was not living up to what I knew was expected of me. On top of that, I had been in countless living rooms across the country, convincing moms and dads to send their sons to play for me, telling them that they would be getting "the best possible version of this young man at the end of his playing experience."

I wasn't doing that. I was strictly driven by the scoreboard curriculum. I was telling our guys to be humble if the scoreboard said we won and to be resilient if it said we lost. And then I was plugging them back into a rinse-and-repeat process of weights, film, practice, scouting report, weights, film, and gameday. There were no life lessons. There was no framing to help them better themselves as husbands and fathers.

I didn't want to be that person anymore, so I went to see Carli Rohner, who, at the time, was the Title IX Coordinator and Director of the Gender Resources Center at Willamette University. I said, "Carli, I do not want my guys committing these horrible acts. I don't want to be this shallow version of a coach. Can you help me create something better?"

That conversation began the work that would eventually develop into the #TeamsOfMen framework that I have laid out in this book for you. I began to figure out how to teach young men the things that matter much more than ball screen defense, touchdowns, or home runs: how to have emotional fluency and agility, how to have healthy relationship skills, and how to break free from the constraints of socialized ideas about masculinity (like #TheManBox) and be change agents in the battle against gender violence and oppression in all its forms.

It was also when I was able to put a *name* to a *skillset* we coaches must embrace in ourselves so we can teach our players to embrace it: #MirrorTraining, or the art of examining the who/what/when/why of yourself. Who did I engage with? What did I do/say? When did I choose that path? Why did I do that? Questions like these require us to take a look in the mirror (sometimes literally, sometimes figuratively) and demand the best of ourselves. Deploying #MirrorTraining moved me to create the

#TeamsOfMen framework, allowing me to walk down a road I hope you will not only follow but take further than I could ever imagine. As a matter of fact, you'll have opportunities at the end of every chapter to rep #MirrorTraining.

In this book, you can expect to find framework insight unpacking a decade's worth of the proven execution of this process with our team. I'm going to take you from this retelling of my "aha" moment to what the design of a consistent program looks like and, finally, to how this work can become a daily part of what you do. For evidence of success, I will provide real-world stories, testimonials, data, and analytics about why and how this works. I will tell you where to start and what day one looks like to do things the right way.

I want to help you overcome skepticism, and I want to assuage any fears you may have about your ability and responsibility to take this on. I want to give you an emotional intelligence blueprint to help you launch the work correctly. I want to talk to you about the positive ripple effects this work will have, not just in your team room but over the whole campus and in your community. And I want to help you ensure a lasting impact by talking about how to sustain the change for more than one speech, one meeting, one season, to make it the core DNA of your program.

If you embrace #MirrorTraining and the #TeamsOfMen framework and make it a part of your day-to-day regimen, you're going to rediscover why you got into coaching in the first place. Whatever game you coach is neutral about your future and your players' best interests. It really doesn't give a damn about any of you. Any life lessons your players get from the game are solely dependent upon the people around them.

You give the game meaning, you give the game importance, and you provide the life lessons. That's what this book can help you do.

CHAPTER 1

Understanding the Framework and the Actual Opponent

C oach, I want you to envision a plan you've come up with for a big game against a rival. Imagine what you wanted that week from your staff and yourself, the work you did reviewing film and scouting, all to ensure you had a detailed idea of the opponent: what makes them tick, what makes them successful, regardless of the sport.

Now, keep that same mindset of preparation, of "knowing our enemy," so to speak, and apply that to the #TeamsOfMen framework when #MirrorTraining with your players. As I stated in the introduction, what got me to start this work was my core disgust at the thought of men committing violence against women with their words and actions. As I evolved and educated myself, I recognized that the behaviors I wanted my players to avoid, the choices I wanted them to never make, were symptoms of a larger problem. While gender violence and oppression are undeniable realities, I came to see that the root of these issues lies within #TheManBox. This term was first coined by Tony Porter, the founder of A Call to Men, an organization that exists to "raise men's and boys' consciousness about their collective socialization so that they can think critically about how they might be reinforcing or passing on these harmful beliefs and so they can challenge those beliefs in other men."

As I dove into literature and speeches, as I unpacked the educational resources provided to me by various professionals I connected with or discovered, I was exposed to the idea that #TheManBox is the unspoken idea of what our young men are supposed to be, how they're supposed to act, and what they must prove day in and day out to other men to claim their mythical "real man badge."

To be a man, according to #TheManBox, they think they must be emotionless. The great activist bell hooks (a distinguished American author, feminist and social activist renowned for her expertise in feminist theory and cultural criticism) cemented this concept in her book *The Will to Change: Men, Masculinity, and Love,* "The first act of violence that patriarchy demands of males is not violence toward women. Instead, patriarchy demands of all males that they engage in acts of psychic self-mutilation, that they kill off the emotional parts of themselves. If an individual is not successful in emotionally crippling himself, he can count on patriarchal men to enact rituals of power that will assault his self-esteem."

Your players have been raised to believe that they cannot be fluent in emotion, they cannot be able to name emotions, and they damn sure can't express or show emotions because then they are labeled "soft," "weak," or a "pu**y."

Next, #TheManBox requires men to be on the lookout for all the ways we can dominate whatever it is we are doing, whether it's sports, relationships, our careers, or in the classroom. We have to be the ultimate, the best, and not just the best achiever but actively working to destroy all the opposition against us. So, we isolate ourselves and become completely alone. Most of us don't realize this because #TheManBox has convinced us that this state of isolation is how we're meant to exist. We must dominate and control everything by ourselves. That's the only way to be a true man. We also have to be sexually active, with a ton of sexual conquests, and cannot commit to one woman. We need to be out looking for notches in the bedpost.

These are the walls that make up #TheManBox. We must have no emotions, nothing but the desire to dominate. This means we can have no true relationships and don't want connection; we only want to be sexually promiscuous and view women as objects to be conquered. Finally, to seal the walls around us, we must gauge our worth solely in terms of material possessions. How much money do we have? How big is our house? How many cars are in our garages? How many PlayStations, Xboxes, and iPhones do we have? How much stuff have we accumulated? That is the only way to feel good about ourselves—we count up our things. When we think like this, we imprison ourselves in the four walls of #TheManBox.

When you recognize that young men are brought up and socialized into believing this formula, it becomes easy to see that a lot of harmful decisions are due to them striving towards this #ManBox. They are acting according to make-believe scoreboards in their rooms. When they lie down at night, they convince themselves that there's a point total under "Timmy's Man Quest" on the wall that says either, "Today, Timmy, you earned seven points toward manhood," or, God forbid, "Today, Timmy, because you confided in a friend that you were sad, you lost 10 points in manhood because you're soft." On days the fake scoreboard claims they lost man points, they double down on the awful tropes, calling each other "pu**y" or "fa***" and stifling emotion away. Then they rinse and repeat to be sure the scoreboard says they're a man tonight.

The gender violence in the community that launched my #MirrorTraining helped me see the harm caused by striving towards #TheManBox and trying to box yourself into a narrow lens of manhood and what it means to be a man in the 21st century. In many cases, men mistakenly believe that #TheManBox requires them to commit these awful actions. It shapes their mindset and belief systems on relationships and women, leading them into situations where they act in ways that cause harm.

That's the scouting report I adopted. My staff of assistant coaches and I couldn't stop these behaviors if we didn't first help our guys break free from #TheManBox. The symptoms couldn't be avoided if we didn't attack the root cause. We needed to show our guys that the staples of #TheManBox are not only rooted in false beliefs but that they're part of a system that narrows the scope of what men think they can be. Subscribing to #TheManBox shackles your potential, closing the doors on all the places you could authentically show up as a man.

#TheManBox doesn't believe that men can be emotional, provide support, have emotional fluency in committed relationships, or be supportive friends, brothers, husbands, and sons. It doesn't believe that we can exist as part of a team and work towards common goals instead of just individual selfish aims. It doesn't believe that we can be defined by anything other than our material possessions. Actually, #TheManBox is anti-man in that it doesn't think we should be anything more than its narrow definition of masculine.

For example, you'll often hear coaches excuse awful behavior by saying, "Well, you know, boys will be boys." This only reinforces the idea that boys have to fit in this box. By dismissing their behavior in this way and stuffing them in this box, we create a cage that prevents them from becoming the men they can be.

This book is really about anti-#TheManBox work. It's about tearing down #TheManBox walls in the belief systems of the young men in our programs as well as the staff and ourselves, the coaches and leaders. How can we explode out of #TheManBox and chase a positive, reimagined manhood that's authentic to who we want to be, complete with emotion, empathy, and compassion? And once we believe we can, when, where, how often do we expose young men to that work? How many days, how many times, and how long (in terms of hours and minutes) do we need to work at it to unlock that cage?

Numerous professionals (from state agency workers to campus resource coordinators to violence-prevention folks) believe that it takes five "doses," five practices (whether done through reading, speeches, lectures, or group interaction and conversation), to start the process of rooting out and unlearning something. Whatever sport you are in, your players will most likely be with you for four to six months. That gives you plenty of time to find five dose points.

In my ten years of sharing the #TeamsOfMen framework with my college basketball team, we probably dedicated 20 to 30 minutes a week (bi-weekly in the beginning) to this work. Once we fine-tuned the program, we got up to 25 doses a year. Our current partners (middle school, high school, and college programs that do the #TeamsOfMen framework to blow up #TheManBox in their routine rooms) average somewhere between eight to 10 doses a season. That's a lot more doable in most coaches' minds.

I hear your brain turning right now, and it's probably saying something along the lines of, "Hey, Kip, this framework sounds great, but I don't have time for five 60-minute lectures on my calendar." I understand that. I see you, and I hear you. TeamsOfMen is asking you for five intentional space creations this season. A dose doesn't have to be a long speech and presentation. As a matter of fact, lecturing is one of the worst ways to communicate knowledge, especially in the 21st century (Source: Science.org).

That's why I'm giving you the following five best activities you could use right after reading this book with your team. If you want to hit that five-dose number this season, these are five introductions to the framework that launch #MirrorTraining as the norm in your program. They've been proven, not just by me but by the partner coaches who have come to use them. Through a variety of sports and with athletes of many different ages, these five activities have routinely gotten the best feedback and have been best at creating momentum and buy-in from players, which is necessary for coaches to feel comfortable going forward with more learning opportunities.

FIRST DOSE: The first practice is simply called "How Do We Change the World?" Post the question as a prompt, write it on a whiteboard, email it to your team before they come into your team space, or, if you're in the off-season, text it out in a team thread and just ask for responses: "Guys, how do you believe we change the world?" You're launching this because you're meeting players with a universal; very few are going to disagree or counter the idea that the world can be improved.

So, start there and then ask them, "What do you think is the formula for changing the world?" As you go through the discussion, solicit answers from your players. The one answer you might get most from the group, one I imagine you're going to end up sharing with them, is some version of, "Well, Coach, we change the world one person at a time. Whether it's through a book, a speech, the work we do, our business, the career we choose, or our children, we'll change the world one mind at a time."

Then I want you to present this counterargument: "While that's a noble idea, fellas, it's too damn slow. Changing the world one mind at a time is going to take too long. It won't change as fast as we need it to, or even in our lifetimes. So, I would challenge you guys and ask, what do you think about the idea that to change the world in the 21st century, we need to infect one influencer at a time? Why one 'influencer' at a time instead of one 'person' at a time? Because an influencer has the chance to multiply and amplify our work rapidly. And guys, I'm here to tell you that as college football players, as high school basketball players, as club soccer teams, you guys are influencers. In our society today, right or wrong, athletes, male athletes especially, are given a platform of influence. And so, if you are an athlete and are going to be given a platform, why am I not, as your coach, giving you the tools, skillsets, and knowledge needed to make that platform ready to change the world in a positive way? That is why we are doing this #TeamsOfMen program going forward."

The entire roll-out of this activity might take you 15 minutes. If you use a text thread, that'll probably even shave some time off because the kids will have thought about the question and be more readily able to share answers with you immediately. But now you've set the stage for *why* we are doing this work, and you've convinced them it's because we believe in the power of "you."

I've learned that it's best not to accuse people first. It would be a mistake to start by saying, "Guys, we have behavior issues. You all can't be trusted, so I'm going to fix you." Instead, best practice says to meet them in their potential power first. You are stating flatly that as their coach, you believe in a future where they stand in their power and become agents of positivity in their circles and communities.

SECOND DOSE: This one is called "The Power of a T-shirt" activity. Many coaches have "dipped their toes in the water," so to speak, by examining the list below of our mantra t-shirts and finding one that speaks to them and the values of their program. They then pick a day to wear the shirt to a team session. It could be the next post-practice team huddle, post-practice team meeting, or film session, and they mark on their calendar, "That's the day I rock this in front of the guys." Inevitably, when the day comes and the coach wears one of those shirts to practice, they find themselves leading their players in dynamic stretching lines, something every coach in every sport in America does.

Mantra T-shirts:

- Mirror Training In Progress
- Curiosity Is A Superpower
- Unlearning Is Growing
- Vulnerability Is A Connection Point
- Change Starts With Me
- Feel To Fuel
- Self Reflection Self Interrogation=Self Reflection

Let's say the coach is wearing a shirt that says, *"Curiosity Is a Superpower."* In almost every instance, one of their players in the middle of high knees is going to stop, examine their shirt, and say some version of, "Coach, what the hell does that mean?" Boom. The coach now has a conversation starter. Does that mean that there's *instant* learning, and the player will immediately request the same shirt for himself? No, it doesn't. But now they have a different idea. They have a different reflection point. They have a different connection to the word "curiosity." And the coach has done their job for the day. They've hit a connection point that they wouldn't have before.

Every coach reading this has used the power of a t-shirt before because they've put slogans, hashtags, mantras, team credos, and core beliefs on a shirt and asked their players to wear it. We harness the power of shirts all the time.

On the day you wear your shirt, during a post-practice huddle, ask, "Hey, guys, what was the last shirt you wore that you thought was championing a message, a cause, a slogan, or a mindset?" Solicit answers from the room. You'll get versions of, "Hey, Coach, I wore this thing that

I thought was really cool from my favorite team," or "Coach, I wore this thing that I thought was right about a social justice topic I care about." Hell, you might even get, "Coach, I wore our team slogan shirt yesterday." Then ask them to reflect and share their thoughts on the courage it takes for a player to put on something that they know is going to be read or impactful as they walk down the hallway of their school, as they walk the campus of their school, or as they walk through the community.

Ask them, "What statement do you think I'm making by wearing this shirt?" Follow up, after asking them to share in groups or with the team, what statements they think they are making. You most likely will get answers from the guys ranging from "Coach, people gonna look at me funny for sure" to "I think most of them would be confused by the shirt." Then you follow up by saying, "Steel yourselves, gentlemen, to people who are going to *agree* with your statement and most importantly, people who are going to *disagree* with your statement." You now have prime real estate to onboard tactics and ways you want them to behave in the face of disagreement, with how to engage in conflict that promotes respectful discussion instead of harmful outrage. That in and of itself is a win for any coach in any sport!

THIRD DOSE: the third best practice to launch this work will take a little bit more time. It's called "The Morning Routine." (Adapted from an exercise shared by Jackson Katz in his book *The Macho Paradox.*) The morning routine requires either a whiteboard, a screen that you've divided into two columns that the whole team can see, or each player with a piece of paper divided down the middle. I know, in the 21st century, not a lot of them will be carrying notebooks around, but a personal piece of paper can create a safer space for your guys to give real answers (as they can protect their answers from each other). Coach, if you've got a large group and want to use partners, you could assign a column to each partner. The morning routine is flexible. Finally, to launch, ask your guys to populate the left side of the column (no matter the setup) with answers to this question: "What do men do in the morning to avoid being victims of gender violence?"

Then ask your guys to populate the right side of the column (no matter the setup) with answers to this question: "What do women do in the morning to avoid being victims of gender violence?" Next, either let kids write their answers down, ask them to come up to the board and fill the column in, or solicit the answers, and then you write them or type them on the board or presentation screen. The important thing is to let them answer. Let them sit in the questions and embrace silence as they think about them (especially the one for the left column regarding male behavior).

Inevitably, you're going to have an exceptionally unbalanced list. On the left side, for men, you're going to have very few things that they think about or believe are required of them to avoid being victims of gender violence. You might get answers like, "Well, Coach, I'm not going to be in prison."

On the right side, however, they're going to imagine what their moms, sisters, girlfriends, cousins, and female friends might have to say. They are going to see a long list of things women have to do just to get through their day due to their fear of being harmed:

"Carry my keys like Wolverine's claws."

"I've got to have mace."

"I'm not going to go out and jog in parks without being in a group."

"I'm not going to go to the club without being in the group."

"I'm going to always buy my own drinks."

"I'm not going to get an Uber without texting my friends first."

You're going to get a long list of things that women have to do.

I want you to ask, "Guys, how does that sit with you? How does this imbalance of stressors, worries, and preparation steps that the women in your life have to take compared to you make you feel?"

Then I want you to ask them, "Who are they afraid of? Why are they worried when they take these steps in their morning routine? Who are they worried about?"

Almost always, the answer will be that they're worried about a man somewhere, somehow, in the course of their day, harming them.

You're going to have some intense self-reflection in these moments where silence will be powerful, and I want you to let your players sit in the realization of what the women in their lives experience and why and who that experience is based on.

Then I want you to drive the following point home: "Gentlemen, here's a sobering truth. All those things, statistically speaking, that women have been told to use to prevent harm to themselves at the hands of a man most likely will *not* prevent a sexual assault because the rates of acquaintance rape, sexual assault from a friend, are through the roof

(Source: aaets.org). So, all these things are done out of fear of the mythical boogeyman. But guys, the movies and comics, all those things that show you someone jumping out of the bushes to sexually assault women, are false. What's really happening is that the men women trust and love are the ones doing them harm."

For far too long, we've asked women to protect themselves from us. In reality, the work that needs to be done is for us to do. How can we learn and unlearn how we behave? How can we be more trustworthy and unpack some of the things we believe about what's going to happen in our relationships? That's why we're taking on Mirror Training this season. That's why I'm a coach who embraces the #TeamsOfMen Framework.

FOURTH DOSE: The fourth best practice is a great advanced lesson that must be paired with number three, "The Morning Routine." It's called the "She's Someone Exercise." In "The Morning Routine," I asked you to tell your players to think about the women they love (their moms, sisters, girlfriends, wives, partners, cousins, and friends). Now we're going to show the players that the idea "I must protect my women" is #TheManBox-tainted framing of why they should care about gender violence.

For the exercise, there's an image that was posted online (you can find it by doing a Google image search of "She's Someone"). If you can't find the exact image, just write the word's below on a whiteboard,"

"She's someone's mom."

"She's someone's sister."

"She's someone's wife."

"She's someone's girlfriend."

Once you've put it where everyone can see it, don't say anything to your guys. Let them talk without any prompts from you (say, two to three minutes). They're going to think, *Oh, here Coach goes again. We're going down this #TeamsOfMen stuff again, and he wants us to think about all the women we care about.*

Now take a marker (if you're typing, just use a capital X) and cross out everything after "She's someone's" on every line.

"She's someone's mom."

"She's someone's sister."

"She's someone's wife."

"She's someone's girlfriend."

Then ask your players, "Why did I do that?"

This was a major self-reflection point for me. Once you see that she's someone and embrace that every human being has intrinsic value and should be valued, you're telling your guys, "We're not doing this just for the people we love. We're doing this because we should be quality human beings who give a damn about everyone we come into contact with, whether we know them or not." From that point on, Coach, you're moving their mindset from, "Oh, I care because of the women I love" to "Nope, now I care because women have value. Human beings have value."

FIFTH DOSE: The last one of your five best practices is called "The Soundtrack to Our Soul." This is best done at the beginning of a season, but it works in the middle of the season as well. To start, you are going to ask the guys to share with you their current favorite song. "What song really gets you ready for practice? What is it you're listening to the most right now?" Give them a day or two to submit answers and build your list of the team's songs. Then, in a sit-down session with the whole team, tell the guys, "Okay, right now, I want you to find the lyrics of the song you've chosen. Use one of the 30,000 different lyric sites online to find the words to your song." Once that's done, go through the lyrics and identify words and phrases in the song that promote violence, racism, sexism, homophobia, sexual conquest, etc. (you can use these categories verbatim or create your own). Do this line by line, all the way through each song.

Finally, add up the occurrences of these words and phrases and turn them into a team document. Tabulate the metrics of the "soundtrack to our soul" as a team. Be sure to include your own favorite song. Then tell the players, "I'm not mandating that we stop consuming certain songs. I'm honestly not. That's not realistic. But I am asking you, if the song you're listening to has this percentage of these things that we all agree we don't want to be a part of, how are you squaring that internally? How are you reflecting and interrogating yourself internally about playing that around each other and people who visit our facility? How is that playing out in terms of your character if that's the input into your mind every morning?"

Do not have pre-prepared answers and new rules for your guys. Kids will see through that. Ask them to reflect. Share with them your song. "I'm a 44-year-old man, and I think this song is awesome. But I have to square right alongside you what its lyrics could mean."

I am the world's longest-living Tupac fan, and I've had to square right alongside my guys and share with them how his hardest-hitting songs (e.g., "Hit Em Up," "Wonder Why They Call U Bitch," etc.) sit when I'm rocking out alone in the Starbucks drive-through versus when I'm in a department hallway with other coaches' offices nearby.

After sharing, you can then advance to more activating questions of potential change: "When we're warming up on the field or court, should these songs be playing? If yes, why? If no, can the edited versions change anything for us? How could those versions be different? How do we stay true to what motivates us but also stay true to who we want to be as a program and what we believe in?"

SUMMARY: You've now been exposed to the five best practices to launch your battle against #TheManBox. These first five doses will take you from meeting your guys to teaching them who they can be as influencers, helping them identify why they want to engage in this work of redefining masculinity and preventing gender violence, and giving them reps in #MirrorTraining. That's your year one, ta-da, and away we go. From experience, these five best practices will not only be an effective launch pad, but they will give you and your staff direct exposure to the skill of embracing *silence* in the moment. Silence will be prevalent and often suffocating, but it will not be because the players are tuning you out. It will be because they are processing heavy ideas for the first time that might reflect poorly on themselves, but you have to let them sit with that for as long as it takes.

Reader #MirrorTraining Challenge (Chapter 1): What tools do you and your staff have to measure your athletes' character? And what are the metric outputs of those tools? No matter what your sport is, I know you have all the stats to measure the effectiveness of athletes on the field or court. But what metrics do you use to measure character? And what tools do you use to measure them? And once you see those metrics, do you like what you see? If you do not have these metrics or tools, how is your program moving men forward in character? How can you say your program teaches character if you do not have metrics to gauge it?

CHAPTER 2

Proof of Concept From 10 Years of Experience

I know coaches reading this book are used to a very simple way of gauging a week's or a season's worth, whether it was successful or not, and that's via the shiny lights on the scoreboard. Whether it's on the football field, the soccer pitch, the baseball field, or the basketball arena, there is a very visible display of lights that says "home" and "visitor," and they tell us if we won or lost. There's a kind of simplicity to that, and there's some comfort in knowing, "I will be able to gauge my efforts tonight immediately after the final whistle blows. I won't have to wait for a report card to come back. I'll know, and then I can make decisions on what to do next."

When you're embracing the #TeamsOfMen framework, number one, the scoreboard will still be there for the on-the-court part of this work. But number two, I need you to retrain your mind and embrace the fact that results will not show up immediately. There's a delayed scoreboard for #MirrorTraining and giving your players that skillset for life.

Football coaches talk all the time about eye discipline. Basketball coaches talk all the time about seeing the play before it happens. This chapter will help you anticipate what it is you're going to look for to prove that the work you're doing is successful, valuable, and energizing to your career.

To begin shaping this new lens, let me take you back to when I shifted to the #TeamsOfMen framework. As I mentioned previously, I was about three or four years into my head coaching career. My early years in the work were focused on building a calendar, building lesson plans, etc. But as my staff and I started to look for ways to gauge effectiveness, I began to ask, "What is the proof that this #TeamsOfMen is working? What's the scoreboard that shows it was good, that your guys are growing from it, that it's worth doing?"

Analytically, we identified a couple of things: Number one, we had three Jostens Trophy finalists in our program. The Jostens Trophy in Division III basketball is awarded to a player of the year nationally (one in both men's and women's basketball), and it isn't just a trophy given out to the highest-scoring player (Source: ODAU.com). High performance is important, and you need to be an all-conference player, but you also need to demonstrate academic excellence and community impact. No other program on the West Coast of the National D3 Circuit could claim that they had three finalists in a decade for this award. We had a total of eight as a program historically (including myself in 2001), but when we used the #TeamsOfMen framework, we had three in 10 years, which is a ridiculously high success rate (Source: wubearcats.com). So, if you're a coach who's moved by statistics, the #TeamsOfMen framework does garner national recognition for guys.

The next factor is retention rates, especially in the early 2020s, square in the middle of the birth of the NIL and transfer portal era in college athletics (coupled with a proliferation of athletes transferring in and out of high schools as well via district of choice provisions and private high schools recruiting more than ever). Program retention rates are a measure of success for our framework. Why would a kid want to join our program, and more importantly, why would a kid want to stay throughout a four-year career in our program? Our retention rates (as measured by matriculation) were consistently in the 80% range. Our rates (and this is not because we played every single player, didn't have depth charts, or didn't pull kids and have accountability for performance on the floor) were high because kids felt valued and seen in our program as human beings.

That is not to say that every single kid looked at me as some kind of messiah or infallible person. No, plenty of kids were still mad at me and the choices I made as a basketball coach (playing time, scheme deployed, etc.), but we created a culture of communication. We created the expectation of vulnerability and transparency. We created the normalcy of engaging in difficult conversations. As kids were feeling the stressors that caused them to leave other programs throughout the country, it was easy for our kids to talk to us and share with us things that maybe they didn't feel able to share in other places. So, retaining players (even though we were not winning championships) at a high clip was proof of concept.

There's also anecdotal evidence of the effectiveness of TeamsOfMen. For example, professors contacted me and said things like, "Hey, Kip, you know what? You have two players in my [insert level and course] seminar class, and they're more willing than anyone else to engage in critical, crucial conversations. I don't know what you're doing with the team, but I just wanted to say those guys are awesome." We got versions of this type of feedback a lot (whether through emails or texts or at lunch in the cafeteria) about kids. If participating and engaging in thoughtful ways in difficult conversations in the classroom is a skillset players take from your program, you've got to give credit for it to the set-up and expectations this framework exposes them to so often.

Listen, like you, we had internal, built-in metrics, different measurables we would use to see if players and the team were growing. We just got better at shaping and creating a similar analysis of this character development work.

Here's another intentional set-up we did to gather data and #feedthefeedback, so to speak. I had attended a coaching clinic at some point and heard high school coach Rahim Tufts (at the time, the head coach at Scappoose H.S. in Oregon) talk about how much mileage he got out of simply stocking a mini-fridge in his classroom with chocolate milk. On game days, his players would all come by at some point during the day to grab a chocolate milk, and he tried to turn as many of those visits as possible into conversations and connection points.

I didn't have a way to afford chocolate milk deliveries, so I adapted the inspiration and put a whiteboard in front of our staff hoops office. Then we told the guys we were launching "Get on the Board Mondays" and "Get on the Board Fridays." All that was required of them on "Get on the Board" days was that they had to sign the whiteboard.

Sometimes, when players signed the whiteboard, they popped their heads into the office and said, "What's up, Coach," to those of us there. Sometimes, they signed it and snuck away with silent footsteps Batman would be proud of. Cool. Great for them. That was fine. But we started to break down the walls associated with going to the coach's office. It's hard for guys to go to the head coach's office, no matter if it's D1 college or middle school, just as it's hard to see a teacher after school. With this program, instead of a player only coming to my office when they were pissed at me or I was pissed at them, they came to my office two times a week, no matter what.

These visits are measurable. You can measure the growth in a player by how often and consistently he follows through on getting on the board on Mondays and Fridays, as well as how long he stays while signing. In addition, you can measure what those "Get on the Board" moments transformed into. Did he start as a guy who, when he signed it, I never saw and never heard? Then did he become the guy who pops his head into the office and says, "What's up, Coach?" And now, when he signs, does he come into the office, sit down, and eat his lunch? That progression is a real example of the growth I saw from players from that simple activity of Getting on the Board. Now, that's not universal to every single player. Of course, it's not, but there was enough of it from year one to year four that it was something we committed to always making a part of our program. And it gave us data points on who the kids were.

Another simple one that sets you up to generate your own proof of concept through data collection is called #TetrisText. #TetrisText was something we started based on the philosophy. I wish I could remember who I gleaned this information from, but you can Google it using "Tetris thinking theory." What the Tetris mindset states is that our brains will continue to stack in patterns. If we feed them nothing but blocks of negativity, our brains will look for negative patterns to fit like the Tetris game, in essence rewiring themselves to fit the effects of long-term, prolonged exposure to those thought processes (Source: Big Think).

We had been losing, so we were concerned (both for the guys and ourselves as staff) that the program was getting bathed in a Tetris-like stacking of "we're going to lose" thinking. So, I tried to disrupt that by giving our brains more than just negativity to digest. Every week, we would assign every player a partner on the team, including the coaches. I might be partnered with a freshman, a junior might be partnered with a senior, etc. Every week, you had a new partner. Then we would send out a question for the week (we would send out the email listing partner assignments and a question every Sunday evening). Maybe it was, "What was the most positive thing that happened to you today?" or maybe it was, "Who made you laugh today?" One week, it could be, "What habit did you start this week that helped you through the week?" and the next, "Who impacted you positively this week?" We were trying to ask them questions that would reconfigure the Tetris programming in their minds from negativity to possibility, from "woe is me" to hope and potential in their everyday lives.

In addition, we practiced sharing our answers with one another. I'd text you the answer to my Monday question, and you would text me your answer. At the end of the week, we'd have five answers from one another. Each partner would have to email me, saying, *"Hey, here's my partner's #TetrisText week of hope,"* or *"Here's my partner's #TetrisText week of positivity."* Then I would add them to a database with every kid's answers.

About every six weeks, I would send out to every player via email something like, *"Hey, man, I know you might be struggling in school, you might be struggling with your shot, and we might be in the middle of a losing streak, but remember, good things have been happening to you as well. Let's keep fighting. Let's stay resilient."* Then I'd give them six weeks of their own words of what was positive in their day, of what was refueling and building hope in their day.

By doing #TetrisText, I learned things about my players that I would never have learned if we hadn't asked them to share in this fashion. They learned things about each other that they never would have known without Tetris. And this all played into and was part of the work of blowing up #TheManBox. Remember, #TheManBox tells me not to know anything about you. #TheManBox box tells me not to share anything with you. #TheManBox tells me not to try to build connections with you but to build ways to dominate you. With the #TetrisText process, we tried to show the players how to create and foster genuine relationships. We tried to show them the benefits of transparency and vulnerability. And we tried to build emotional resilience and reshape negative thinking.

So much of it was measurable. I could use it as an accountability tool (e.g., "We're running because two guys didn't turn in #TetrisText this week"), and I could use it as a show of community ("Look at this word cloud of stuff we shared with each other last week. That's a family man. That's vulnerability. Proud of you guys"). I can tell a player, "Hey, man, no, you actually have grown. Look where you were in the struggle you had to answer #TetrisText in November. Look where you are *now* in January. Look at the things going on for you. I see it, and now I can share that with you."

Let's pivot now and look at ourselves as coaches executing the sessions. When you're activating the #TeamsOfMen framework and actually living it and coaching it, and you're intentional about finding ways to instill it in the plan every day, you are fueling your capacity as a coach as well. We've all struggled in a season. We've all been on losing streaks. We've all been in spaces where it was hard for us to think about going to practice that day, where it was hard for us to think about finishing off the week, thinking, *I'm drained. I'm tired.* Those are real pain points for coaches.

But when you are coaching to this framework, and you're not driven by scoreboard curriculum, you find yourself recognizing so many more moments where the players are the ones fueling you. There are so many more moments where you can tell a kid, "You know what, man? I see you." How many times, Coach, have you said, "Guys, I love everybody here, but I cannot show you how much I value you in equal playing minutes for everyone. I cannot show you how I value you in the snaps you get. I cannot show you how I value you in the at-bats you get. There's a limited amount of those resources, and we've got to put the best people in the best positions, and sometimes, you're going to be left out. But I do see you. I do value you."

When you can't value them, it drains you. It's a draining moment when a kid feels invisible, and you know it. It's a draining moment when you know the kid doesn't believe that you value them as a person or as a player or that they don't feel wanted in the program. When you coach to the #TeamsOfMen framework, you have so many more touch points with your players, whether it's the Get on the Board moments, the #TetrisText reflections, or the comments in the meetings when they're sharing and reflecting on all these topics that have nothing to do with your sport. These are all opportunities for you to say, "Hey, you know what? I heard your voice today, man. That's a big step for you. Congrats. You hadn't shared in #TeamsOfMen for a couple of months. That's awesome. Thank you for that." There's another data point. There's another spot in that kid's day where you can show them true visibility.

I do believe that, as coaches, we owe every single player in our program visibility daily. We do not owe them mobility in their job, in their role. We do not owe them a starting position. No, but we owe them "I see you" moments because every single young athlete, if you look at all the studies, is desperate for visibility and the feeling that someone truly knows him (Source: equimundo). This work allows you to fulfill that need.

Next, let me share another great story of proof of the work, of a time I had to embrace this work when I was at my lowest. So, when I got let go from being the head coach at my alma mater after 15 years (25 total years as a player, assistant coach, and then the head), it wounded my soul. It was a devastating day I most likely will never forget. Luckily, I got invited, alongside my longtime quality-control coach Kevin MacRae (who'd been with me for a decade), to one of our former players' weddings. It was in May, about a month and a half after I'd been let go, and I was still struggling. I won't sugarcoat it; I was down—on myself, on not being able to complete the tasks and the goals I'd set out for the scoreboard and winning at Willamette—and lacked all belief I had done anything of value in my time there.

The groom had six of our guys in his wedding party, and four more were just invited, so it was almost like a team reunion. All those kids had gone through the #TeamsOfMen framework and the #TeamsOfMen program with us. And without even knowing it, those kids saved me. It was the groom and his bride's day, and I'm sure they didn't say, "Hey, let's go pump up my old college coach's self-esteem," but the way those kids spoke to me and Kevin and engaged with us and just the camaraderie of real family, real bonding, real brotherhood, seeing how they still treated each other within the framework of what we had hoped to instill in them, was refueling for me.

I left there on a high I hadn't felt since the firing, and I know it was because those kids were fluent in the work. I had struggled, thinking, *Damn, was #TeamsOfMen part of the reason I was let go?* This wedding convinced me that #TeamsOfMen was the only reason I was able to coach for so long without the success I wanted on a scoreboard. I had shown up every day, energized, because we were doing the framework, because we had invested in #MirrorTraining.

Lastly, this work can ease some of the tension that exists between parents and coaches, especially high school coaches. It's inevitable that, at some point, you will have strife with a parent or two. As coaches, we can never love their children the way they do. It's impossible. They can never coach the team, prioritizing its needs over the needs of their children the way we have to. That's an impossible task. What we can do is find common ground and admit that, when it comes to the basketball, football, soccer, or baseball part of this, we will never find true alignment. It's just not built into the cards. Where we can find common ground is with the human being we share because we give a damn about their kids, and so do they. Can we find common ground on the growth of his character? Can parents trust that we have that in mind? Can we go forward knowing that the young man is getting better, regardless of what happens with him as an athlete, because we will probably never agree on that? Some of our partner programs have found success with that. That doesn't mean there isn't still some strife about playing time or minutes, but there's been an ease of tension between coaches and parents.

I had a senior breakfast a couple of years ago, and I was worried about discussing each senior's contributions to our program and the season they'd had (all in an effort to celebrate them). You interact with parents at these events, and I was nervous about it because I had taken the starting job from one particular senior. He was still a contributor off the bench, but obviously, as a senior, it's a tough pill to swallow when the starting job's given to somebody else in your final season, especially in college because for a lot of kids, that's going to be their final year of competitive basketball.

When we finished honoring each senior and were milling around, eating and chatting, I saw this senior's father approaching, and I thought, "Oh, boy, this might be the beginning of this thing going sideways." But the dad came up to me with tears in his eyes and said, "You did everything you promised you would do for him as a person. He's a better man because of the program you guys run."

That emotional reaction was not because of some set of rules I mandated that his son follow for four years. It was because we told him (I vividly remember the in-home visit because the meal that he and his wife provided was so great) during that recruiting visit that we would create an intentional space every single season his son played with us to help him grow in his humanity, to find a path for him and set him on a journey to become the best version of himself. I confidently told them in the living room, "Hey, I can't make a lot of promises, but I don't want to do that because then I'm a car salesman, and I don't want to be a car salesman to you. This is your son, and we're talking about his future. But I can promise you that no one else in the country will put him through this intentional time and this routine to think about who he is as a man. I can't promise him All-American status. I can't promise him points per game. I can't promise him championships. It's just not part of the deal, but I will promise him this."

At the end of that young man's senior year, at the senior breakfast celebration, the dad validated one of the reasons we want everyone to embrace this framework. He saw the value, despite the on-court demotion and diminishment of his son as an athlete, and felt that we had followed through in our promise to help his son grow as a person. That was a powerful confirmation of what this work can do.

Reader #MirrorTraining Challenge (Chapter 2): This harkens back to my wedding story, but I want you to ask yourself, Coach, when was the last time you connected with a former athlete? Think back to that setting. Now, first of all, if you haven't connected with a player who has moved on from your program, that is something you need to address. But let's assume you have. What was the setting? Was it on the phone, or did you meet up for coffee or dinner? Where'd you see this player? What was the conversation like? What did they want to share with you, or what did they want to reminisce about?

If you've used the #TeamsOfMen #MirrorTraining framework, I'd imagine that a lot of their recollections were lessons and resilient moments that you all got through or learned together. I imagine very little of it was about the last time you drew up a cool play. Very little of it was about the skills or techniques of the game. I'd imagine a lot of it was about the skills you gave them for life. And if you're not in that moment, if you don't have that, this is the challenge for you after you've done this #MirrorTraining: start to build that type of relationship.

When I was let go, none of my guys texted me about the timeout draws I did in January in one of their college basketball seasons. None of them texted me about the shell drill we ran. They all texted, called, or emailed me about the life lessons and the way I'd made them feel. Those were the moments that lasted and resonated.

CHAPTER 3

Starting the Work

As mentioned earlier, coaches often tell me, "Kip, I don't know where to begin." I can feel their stress when they say, "When do I do this, what if I start in the wrong place, Kip? You're telling me about blowing up #TheManBox. You're telling me I'll be helping my men prevent gender violence. You're telling me about helping them embrace #MirrorTraining. It's a lot, man. I don't even have a launch point." Calm down, Coach. I want to reemphasize that this is not the exhaustive list of things that you think it is.

Start here. Look at your calendar, Coach, as it stands today. Look at how detail-oriented you already are. Stand in your power as someone who schedules and prioritizes at a high level. A lot of us are probably high D-type folks (in the DISC assessment—which helps identify our preferred communication style—be it Dominance, Influence, Steadiness, or Conscientiousness—enabling us to adapt and interact more effectively with others based on this self-awareness), and we've already got our calendars set for the next six months minimum. Whether that calendar looks like my old college coach's (and it's on these eight-by-11-inch pieces of paper with the smallest handwriting known to man used to smash in all the bullet points possible) or it's set up digitally in Google Calendar, I know it's alive and well somewhere. On that calendar, you've got all these different versions of the day-to-day interaction opportunities with players listed. And your guys know where to go to find out what the hell they're supposed to be doing on any given day for the foreseeable future. It's September, and you already know where you need to be in January. I know that's where you're at because that's where I was as a planner for 15 years.

So, look at this beautiful calendar. Where in that calendar can you already see moments where you and your team are going to be circled up as a group? Where are the group sessions, the group meeting times in your season? How long are they? No matter what sport you coach, there are usually films, post-practice circle-ups, weight sessions together, or pre-game meetings where the group assembles. Those setups tend to run anywhere from five to 30 minutes, depending on what is planned. So, if you look there, you already have existing setups for your guys to give you their full, undivided attention. They are already on your calendar.

Now, what would it take to use some of those for TeamsOfMen and #MirrorTraining? What would it really cost you as a program? Do a cost-benefit analysis, and I bet you realize that transforming 15 minutes at the end of weights into a #MirrorTraining discussion would probably not cost a lot. We're not even talking about having to transform an entire segment at a time. Just add 10 minutes to one of them for #TeamsOfMen framing and add it only once every two weeks.

Suddenly, you have "the when" taken care of on your calendar. You already know, and you've already made it clear to your guys (by putting it on the official calendar), that this is *important* to you, and it's going to exist in the culture going forward. Depending upon your choices, you'll start to have players with the expectation that "film is where we gather together and talk about Coach's important stuff," "Our pre-practice circle is where coach always talks about his #MirrorTraining," or, as some of our partners have done, "Hey, before our team weight training, we always gather in the middle of the weight room." There's already ample time on your calendar for this work. Let's put that worry to bed!

Next, let's dive into the what of this work and how it isn't 200-page studies or three-day doctoral dissertation presentations. Often, a lot of this work is just a question or a statement you make or write on the board or text to your players' phones that you want everyone to consider. Much of the time, you are asking them to sit in silence and reflect, and then you progress to talking about it, grappling with it, and arguing about it.

You don't need to have bullet-point speeches that will be remembered for eternity. You need to have your players circled up together. We have already established how to accomplish that. Then, you need to have something to digest together. You don't even need to have an exact takeaway in mind when you launch these conversations. Some of the most powerful moments happen when you sit in the circle with them, shoulder to shoulder, unpacking this work together.

Let me give you a low-stakes example of how a coach in a high school football program started. He said, "Kip, I'm going to start a captain's lunch on Mondays. We're going to call it #TeamsOfMen Mondays, and my captains, there are six of them on this particular football team, will bring their lunch to my room on Mondays during the season. I will need questions from you, Kip, or I'm going to have questions that I'm just going to ask while we eat together. Sometimes, I'm going to ask them questions about what they're experiencing as men growing up in the world. Sometimes, I'm going to ask their opinions on current events happening in our school, our community, or in the sports world, and we're just going to talk." Kids are always bound to feel less stress when they are eating. They're more likely to bond and discuss food. And so are you. It's a time-honored tradition across cultures, sharing while eating.

That's an example of where to start this work: on a Monday, during lunch, or you could launch a once-a-week breakfast session. If your program has team dinners (a lot of coaches do a great job of building camaraderie through team dinners), create the norm that before everyone has dessert, you always discuss a #TeamsOfMen topic or have a #MirrorTraining session. Combining any of these ideas with the calendar creation we did earlier in this chapter gives you a ready-to-roll launch plan.

Now, let me share a "don't do this" and tell you what I messed up in my start so you don't have to repeat the error. While I can attest to this false start in the work being rooted in a genuine desire to keep my young men from committing gender violence of any kind, it doesn't diminish the fact that if I had known what I am telling you now, I could have avoided wasting the first months on bad tactics. Remember, a key point in this work that will pop up again and again for you is that intent *never* excuses or frees you from the consequences of impact. Here's how I learned that the hard way.

I started the work by sharing and posting a ton of shocking stats about gender violence and its prevalence on college campuses (you can find up-to-date statistics with a simple Google search). I did so because stats move me. I read a bunch of reports, and I saw the reality of the horrific things happening to women on college campuses across the country in terms of sexual assault, stalking, and a host of other awful, violent acts (Source: rainn.org). So, I shared these verbatim with that first group of players we asked to #MirrorTrain. I said, "Look at this stuff, guys. Young men are doing a lot of terrible things, and dammit, it's not going to be anyone in this program."

One glaring example of these first false starts was a quiz I gave that first group of young men that was full of gotcha questions. I had created a quiz with multiple-choice answers, but I knew that my guys were not going to have a clue about what many of the answers were and were probably going to pick the wrong ones. Hell, I had existed all those years without knowing any of the stats I was now onboarding. And because I was shocked by how little I knew about the realities of gender violence (and male athletes committing harm on campuses), I had taken the embarrassment of not knowing and turned it into a desire to learn more, and I figured my players would, too. So, I designed this quiz for them to fail, something that would, in my mind, rock their world to the point of activation. When they took the quiz, it was purposely designed to make them feel foolish or inadequate in their knowledge. That backfired on me because after they took the quiz, all those things happened, and they felt stupid; they put up a wall for a few weeks afterward. It is never beneficial when starting a dialogue to make someone feel stupid the first time they embrace vulnerability.

In addition to this bad quiz start, I did other versions of "don't do this, don't do that, don't do this, don't do that" pleas, and they didn't take hold, either. This was not because I had a legion of perpetrators in my team room but because the numbers and stats represented acts that were so horrific (sitting atop both the violence pyramid and the rape culture pyramid— you can Google Image search *"Rape Culture Pyramid"* and/or *"Violence Culture"*) that it was very easy for the young men in my room to dismiss me with, "Coach, I do agree that those numbers are bad, but I will never do those things." It was too easy for the young men to disassociate from the stats because they weren't rooted in things they could identify with or even envision themselves participating in.

Those first sessions fell flat with a majority of my players despite the facts being proven and the accuracy of the numbers. I had to shift my focus from the acts themselves to the belief system of the men who chose to commit them. We had to reorder our roll-out and say, "We're going to reshape who you believe you need to be as a man. We're going to rebuild what you think exhibits positive masculinity, which will require us to blow up #TheManBox." Once we did that, once we engaged in discussions on defining masculinity and sharing how restricting it can be to a young man's authentic self and how it affects their relationships, behaviors, and decisions, it was easier for them to reflect, learn, and see themselves engaging in those things day to day.

I even shifted that quiz and turned it into an anonymous pretest where there was no way they could be embarrassed in front of each other but could answer truthfully. I took away the multiple-choice answers and just asked them to reflect on different aspects of the work and tell me what exposure, experiences, previous learning, and prior knowledge they might have. As we (the coaching staff) went forward with this new pretest, we had a better idea of where our incoming recruits were and where we needed to launch them in the #TeamsOfMen #MirrorTraining process. Each class gave us a better snapshot of their experiences and education with the subject matter we wanted to use, and that allowed them to share their truth honestly in our spaces without it being weaponized against them.

Then I doubled down on the impact by talking about how #TheManBox policing had existed in my own life. I doubled down by embracing my vulnerability, and this helped me work even more powerfully because once I engaged in vulnerability, I gave the guys permission to engage in it, too. I modeled it. What do I mean by that? It involves you as the coach (and this is a heavy lift and ask for you) believing the benefit will outweigh the stress and the angst you're feeling about sharing with your athletes moments in your life when you failed.

As I mentioned before, when you are sitting in a circle with your players, not in front of them, and saying, "Guys, let me unpack for you the ways I, your coach, came up short as a husband, father, son, and friend. I know you see me as the head coach, and I've got the whistle, and I have all the plans, and supposedly, I have all the answers. Well, let me tell you, I don't. That's right, I'm sharing this person you might not know very well because you only know me as 'Coach.' Let me introduce you to myself and how I, the husband, messed up here, how I, the father, messed up here, how I, the friend, struggled with this, and how I, the son, struggled with this."

By sharing your vulnerability, not only are you getting some of the benefits of this work via self-reflection and self-interrogation to level up your own self-awareness, but you're showing your players how to do it for themselves. You're showing them that in this space and with this team, they are going to be able to unpack and share personal things. You're showing them that transparency is sharing something accurately that's happened to you, while vulnerability is sharing something that somebody can use to hurt you once they know it.

One of the most powerful lessons in the early years of rolling out this work was when I detailed the way I used to live in #TheManBox and how I would police my teammates when I was a high school and college player. I was always intentionally posted up in the back of the bus because that was my place to dominate and control the scene, so to speak. I would dominate the scene by pointing out the flaws in all my vulnerable teammates and making everyone else laugh. And these flaws that I pointed out (like who or what sexual experiences people didn't have, or who or what things people did or didn't do physically with girls on dates) were all #TheManBox-driven and awful ideas about what relationships should be.

If I knew you were struggling in a class, weren't playing well, or air-balled a crucial shot, whatever, I was going to weaponize it. All those things that I would point out made me "Kip, the funny storyteller guy," the guy who made everybody laugh. It was all at the expense of my teammates. But what I knew deep down then (and shared with my players later) was that I was terrified that my teammates would discover that all the flaws of others I made fun of also existed in me. It was my own truth I was desperate to hide. I didn't have relationships with girls. I hadn't had a sexual experience. I'd just struggled in a game and missed four free throws. Whatever the flaw might be, I was going to make sure (because #TheManBox told me that I had to dominate and never show weakness) that I pointed it out in everyone else first. #TheManBox told me that if I told the masses of the flaws in others, I would stay on top and never be exposed myself. I did that in the back of the bus, and I was the best at it.

I told my players these stories, saying, "You can ask the alumni that come around our program who played with me, and they'll probably all tell you, 'Kip was this great storyteller.' I'm here to tell you, guys, I was this great storyteller, but it was all at the expense of people I called teammates, of people I called brothers, people I called friends. And now that I'm in my 40s, I'm ashamed and sorry for what I did and how I lived. I lived this lie so you don't have to repeat it."

That's another example of how the work doesn't require you to read three novels. The work requires you to be willing to unpack the novel of your own life with your players. Once you do, you not only help them write a better version of their own lives, but you give them permission to share previous chapters of theirs that they wouldn't have done before.

When you're doing this, when you're in these circles and begin the work, as mentioned earlier, silence is processing; it's not ignoring or being distant. As a coach, you're used to saying something in practice or a game, and it happens immediately. "Jump to it, boys. Get to it. Blah, blah, blah." I whistle, I clap, and everybody runs. In this work, sometimes, people are stuck in their processing, and that's okay. Sometimes, people fall into a fight, flight, or freeze response. You're asking them to recall things that they've pushed down, and some of those responses are to flee or freeze in it, and they go quiet. This should not be taken as an insult. It's actually an acknowledgment of how powerful the moment has been. This work doesn't always lead to verbal responses in front of the team. Everyone in your program will grow in their willingness to share.

Remember that this work is requiring them, for the first time, to take a critical lens not only to themselves but to the people they love and respect.

You're asking them to re-examine their dads, brothers, coaches, uncles, teachers, mentors, and friends. They love these people and the words they shared with them, the lessons they shared with them, and their experiences with them. So, it's going to take a while before they're willing and able or even capable of articulating what they're feeling about those people or themselves. It's a heavy moment, so embrace the silence and build different methodologies and permissions for people to grow into the power of their words.

Lastly, if you're still worried about when and how to START, let me share this: that fear is why #TeamsOfMen exists in the first place. One of the ways a lot of teams and coaches find comfort, in the beginning, is by bringing me in personally to launch and set the table for them with their players. We have a set of 45- to 60-minute keystone speeches that show your young men just what this #MirrorTraining stuff is. Through these keynote topics (like "Who Taught You, Examining Your Professors of Manhood" and "Bridges and Platforms, How You as a Male Athlete Can Change the World for the Better"), we bring the young men into the discussion from a place of strength and a belief in their power rather than from a place of accusation or belittling of who they are.

We believe this setup is best because it allows coaches to view the work from the vantage point of their players. By setting the stage, we prime your guys for your follow-up and intentional space creation long after we're long gone. The feedback from coaches on the workshop has validated that idea, as it's been filled with comments like, "You know what, Coach? The players said, 'Hey, remember that speaker we had? Is this why we're having this conversation today?' or 'Oh, this is because of that Kip guy that came in and talked? That's why you have us doing these meetings every two weeks, right?'" It has been a successful way for coaches to overcome anxieties about the work. Allow us to do the beginning, and then we can pass the baton to you.

Reader #MirrorTraining Challenge (Chapter 3): Think about a relationship in your life that you would call vital to your growth as a person. Have you shared that relationship, and why do you consider it vital with your guys? If you have, ask other people on your staff (and then eventually the players) to share about the people who have been vital to their growth.

If you haven't shared, why not? There's power in such a positive story. This is an easy place for you and your players to start sharing. Remember, we want to meet people where they are before we ask them to move off that spot. This is a lower-stake share, but it lays the groundwork for critically examining the experiences you've had with people.

CHAPTER 4

Beyond Rules

Stop me if you have had these thoughts while reading the first few chapters of this book:

Well, you know, we have standards, Kip.

Hey, you know what, Kip, all these things you're talking about, I already have a set of rules.

Oh, Kip, you know what? We have signs posted up in our locker room. They say things we believe in, the core values of our program.

Well, Kip, they signed a paper for us. They signed a standards and policies paper for us, so we're kind of addressing these things already.

Am I correct that at least one of those crossed your mind? It's okay. I get it. You're not the first coach who's thought about those things when exposed to #MirrorTraining and the #TeamsOfMen framework. But none of those 'rules' you have now are actually going to move the needle. In fact, many of them are insufficient and constitute performative lip service. I started my head coaching career as a guy who had the rules and standards up but didn't have the substance, the program, or the process behind them to actually change behavior in my team room.

In my first two or three years as head coach (I got the job when I was 29 years old), I dove into Pete Carroll's book *Win Forever*. The book implores you, especially young coaches working in their first programs, to create a visual representation of your foundation and have a physical document with your foundational core beliefs listed. I followed the rules of the book and what Coach Carol said and created what my staff and I called our covenants, our foundation. I had this visual of three pillars: men, family, and legacy (I actually carried those terms throughout my coaching career). I wrote out these long bullet lists of what "men" meant to me, what "family" meant to me, and what "legacy" meant to me. But even as a relatively young head coach, I was still a gray-hair in the eyes of my players, and the words I used to describe these pillars of behavior (that would govern who we were as people in our program) meant little to them.

As I evolved in the #MirrorTraining process and applied the #TeamsOfMen framework in my coaching, I realized it would ultimately be more powerful (and likely to get more buy-in from the players on embracing this foundational document as a behavior guide) if they could contribute input with these covenants, namely what each column header meant and what it looked like to live it in our program every year. We even evolved from the image of pillars to coils.

The players' input and the resulting discussions helped us recognize that the strongest version of our foundation needed to be able to contract and expand as our real-world experience demanded. We realized pillars have a crumbling point. You can break a pillar with enough pressure. At a certain point, it will crumble. But a coil, a spring, can contract and expand depending upon the world's pressures.

This process taught me the limits of "rules and a code" if the coach simply orders them. You need buy-in, and you get it when players feel they have a voice in the process. This allows you to be less of an authoritarian figure and more of a collaborator toward a shared vision of what it is to be part of the program and who you, your staff, and your players want to be as humans.

Let me frame the limitations of one "rule" in basketball (you can flip this to soccer and football as well because they have turnovers in their games, too). My staff and I believed (I think it's probably a universal truth) that turnovers in basketball cost games. "Turnovers are killing us" is a true statement. They will cause you to lose.

With that framing, when you get to your first practice of the year, your 30th practice of the year, your 100th practice of the year, you know you will be telling your players how to avoid turning the ball over, and none of your practice plans will not include some version of building skills to avoid turnovers. You never settled for a single practice at the beginning of the season where you said, "Stop turning the ball over," and then didn't schedule any more practice segments on the topic for the rest of the year.

As a matter of fact, Coach, I know exactly what you would do to prevent turnovers because I did the same over 20 years of coaching. You would dive into film with your staff and players, individually, in groups, and as a team, to find the exact actions (the traveling, the errant passing, the illegal screens, the fouls) that are causing turnovers. You'd tag those first. "Here are the turnovers. Here's what they are. This is what they look like." Then you'd say, "You know what? I think these are the skills we're lacking that are leading to those actions. Maybe we have poor ball-handling ability, which is leading to some of our double dribbles and carries. Our footwork development is also poor, which is leading to our travels. We have bad vision and read progressions, which is leading to passes getting stolen. And we don't have good two-foot stops, which is why we're getting a ton of illegal screens and charges because we're not truly stopping."

You would not only know what turnovers look like, but you would also know the lacking skillset that is causing those turnovers to happen. Then you and your staff would go about the work of creating segments in practice for the week, month, and season, thinking, "If we do these drills and these segments and these sessions in practice, we'll build our skillsets, and if we build the skillsets, we will begin to eliminate some of the turnovers that are killing us in games." I think that is exactly what you should do and exactly what coaches for generations have been doing.

My issue is that in using that process to fix an issue in team performance, you are admitting that there needs to be an intentional, tiered progression to onboard skillsets. Agreed! But we're somehow NOT doing that when it comes to onboarding skillsets that are costing our kids off the floor. In some cases, depending on the severity of their actions and behaviors, it will cost them their futures. It will cost them the version of life that they are capable of. So, why are you settling for simple one-offs and saying, "Well, I told my guys that they were to be respectful in this program," or "Kip, you know, we signed it. We signed a document once that says they should be good people." We need to admit the hypocrisy that we've been living with when we design month-long calendars around skillset growth for competitions but do not do the same for skillset growth in who they are as people and as men.

Let's go to the turnover analogy again. Say you're getting reports, whether in middle school, high school, or college, that your players aren't respectful in class, the hallways, or the cafeteria. Teachers are telling you that your guys are making inappropriate comments to protected groups (women, LGBTQ students, special needs groups) and are bullying freshmen (Source: osu.edu). These things are the equivalent of turnovers. These are disrespectful acts. Just as we ascribed traveling to poor footwork, we would say, "We have low emotional fluency in our team room," or "We do not have a strong idea of what healthy manhood is, and our relationship skills are in the toilet."

We would tag #TheManBox as contributing to those deficiencies: "We have low emotional fluency, unhealthy ideas of manhood, and poor relationship skills, and it's all rooted in #TheManBox. That's leading to the disrespectful acts and inappropriate comments targeting protected groups and the bullying of freshmen." Instead of building practice drills around this, we would know we need #TeamsOfMen framework sessions. That's beyond simply having rules. It's activating learning and having conversations that build decision-making paradigms and belief systems that will lead our kids to be better versions of themselves.

One of my big issues in doing this work (hopefully, this isn't a trap that you're falling into, Coach) is hearing, "Well, you know, we have a culture already, Kip." I've noticed when working with different teams in different places that everyone wants to be about culture and character until it involves assessing and addressing the way your players are treating others, especially women and the younger, less popular, or less capable athletes on your roster. In a lot of ways, coaches have used broad terms like "respect" and "leadership" as shields against taking on work they are afraid to do. If you go past leadership or culture building, you're going to have to turn over your own rock. You're going to have to embrace the formula of self-reflection plus self-interrogation equals self-awareness. And when you turn that rock over, you're going to find how #TheManBox is influencing you. Or you're going to find that you're so immersed in #TheManBox, your team is so immersed in #TheManBox, it's going to be a heavy lift to break free from it. I've found that it prevents coaches from starting this journey— from starting this work.

I'm here to tell you that it is possible. It's a heavy lift, but it is doable. And your players and you will benefit from doing more than going to a leadership convention one time. You cannot lead a locker room in positivity if you are rooted in #TheManBox. You cannot galvanize a group of individuals behind a common cause if you or the leaders on your team are rooted in #TheManBox and are simply chasing dominance. Often, when you go to these leadership conventions, you're trying to find better ways to gain obedience. Embracing the #TeamsOfMen framework and doing the #MirrorTraining regularly with your players is not chasing obedience. It's building decision-making paradigms for autonomous, independent human beings, allowing them to embrace their agency. That type of player you can trust to align their behavior with the values you promote.

Remember, Coach, the goal of this work is not seasonal character. Seasonal character is when your players follow your code, your bullet points, or the signs in your room because they want to play on Friday, because they want to play on the road trip, not because they've actually done the work of redefining themselves in a healthier way. Once your season is over and they no longer have to be around your signs or your lists, they go back to their true behavior.

You don't want seasonal behavior. You don't want to build systems rooted in "Can I just get him to the playing surface on Friday?" We are asking you to believe that if you've exposed him to thoughts and ideas that allowed him to unlearn toxic ideas of manhood and rebuild an authentic version of himself, you can trust, his mom can trust, and the community can trust him when he's 23 years old at a bachelor party in Las Vegas. You can trust that he will have the skillsets to navigate that scene with the right amount of fun and enjoyment, as well as care and respect.

Reader #MirrorTraining Challenge (Chapter 4): I want you to list all the skillsets and requirements of your sport. Then tag the ones that are most vital to the scoreboard that says you won at the end of the game. (For example, as a basketball coach, I might list my top three as turnovers, shot selection, and rebounding.) Then I want you to list out when and how you addressed those skillsets with your staff and team. Did you settle with any of them, giving a one-time speech or statement to them and calling that "coaching"? I bet the answer is NO and that you devoted multiple practices to those skillsets.

Now I want you to take a look at your list and remember that you probably embrace the "show me, don't tell me" ideology in your program. You require your players to prove who they are by competing, not boasting. What is the work you've done for them as people? What is the work you've done with the skillsets required to become quality human beings? Where is your list, and what time segments have you set aside for those?

CHAPTER 5

Five Common Doubts

As I travel the country, both physically (getting on planes and going to different schools and athletic departments) and digitally (via social media, YouTube, and email), I hear common reasons why coaches can't start the work I champion. This chapter is dedicated to the five self-diagnosed limitations that coaches tell me prevent them from onboarding the framework.

Number one, I often hear various versions of, "Kip, I don't know this stuff. Kip, I'm terrified to say the wrong thing." On that point, know that I, too, started off terrified of my lack of knowledge. Hell, I was a business economics major in college, and I have a master of arts degree in teaching. I do not have a degree in gender studies or diversity, equity, and inclusion (DEI). I do not have a doctorate in violence prevention. But the work doesn't require those things. It requires a coach's willingness to learn and unlearn alongside his players. It involves onboarding and embracing the skillsets of vulnerability and curiosity to drive the work. You can access the experts and the technical knowledge AFTER you decide to embrace those things.

If you're at a college, walk across campus to the Office of Gender Resources or the Title IX DEI office (just like I did on the campus where I was employed) and ask for help. Put up a big sign on your head that conveys you are lost and need a roadmap. Some professionals have been doing this work for their entire careers and are more than willing and capable of helping you along your path. All this requires for you to actually know is that you want your players to be part of the solution and not the problem. That's it. "I want my guys to be pillars of values-aligned behavior. I want my guys to be pillars of a re-imagined manhood and a positive masculinity." That's the end of the requirement. Then go about embracing the scientific mind, embracing curiosity, learning things, and being vulnerable enough to unlearn things, and do these things alongside your guys.

The second common doubt or reservation I hear is, "I just don't have the time." Coaches say, "I already have a full plate between practice and game planning, scheduling, fundraising, academic monitoring, dealing with alumni, parent relations, etc. I'm too busy." I do not doubt the packed status of their calendars. I know they're busy. I lived the life. I lived the grind. I recognize the pulls on your day as a coach, the numerous hats you will show up wearing in your time at your facility, and all the requirements you have at home as a husband, father, friend, or son. But I ask you to consider my belief that all of those requirements, all of those things that are sucking time from you, every one of them would be improved by a team of players (plus a staff of coaches) acting more often than not with values-aligned behavior.

You can't claim that your calendar is full of the real stuff. "Kip, I've got real things to worry about as a coach." "Kip, I've got these priorities that we have to have. And this coaching framework, #MirrorTraining, doesn't fit with them." You cannot claim that when all of those things we just mentioned fall by the wayside (and, in many cases, won't even take place) if your players do not have values-aligned behavior and are poor decision-makers off the competition surface.

Your players will not make it to practice. They will not be part of your game planning. They will not be at the games. You will not be able to spend as much time as you want creating awesome practice plans, designing effective scouting reports, attending fundraising events, or being out in the community if your players are committing harm on your campus or in the community. Your academic monitoring will go through the roof because players will not be performing in the classroom. Your alumni and parent relations will be in the toilet because of actions your players are taking that don't sit well with your alumni base or parent group. Honestly, you'll be in more parent meetings because their children will be making poor decisions due to behaviors that you've failed to help them unlearn. Your fundraising will be in the toilet because you will not have community support and belief in the character of your players in your program.

So, you cannot say, Coach, that you are prioritizing real things on your calendar instead of the #TeamsOfMen framework instead of chances for your guys to do #MirrorTraining. You can't say that the extra 15 minutes at shootaround you chose over blowing up #TheManBox was the best thing to prioritize. If you don't do that work, all the other things that you have on your calendar simply won't happen or will happen at a much worse level than you want them to—not to mention that much of what we've talked about in the previous chapters only takes 20 minutes every other week.

The third of the five most common doubts I get exposed to is, "My guys don't want me to talk about this," or "Kip, my guys and their parents don't want me to dive into these topics, and besides, they are learning this stuff from other places." That is factually inaccurate. Every study, especially two major studies released in the last year and a half, one from Equimundo and another from It's On Us, paint a picture of men (teenage through early adulthood) desperate for someone to engage in conversations with them on consent, healthy manhood, and creating relationships. Equimundo is an applied research organization dedicated to achieving gender equality and social justice by transforming intergenerational patterns of harm and promoting care, empathy, and accountability among boys and men throughout their lives. It's On Us, founded in September 2014, is the nation's largest nonprofit program dedicated to college sexual assault prevention, training a national network of student-led campus chapters to become peer educators and conducting research to expand the field of knowledge on violence prevention.

A study released this year by Harvard's Making Caring Common Project pointed out that young men in high school report not learning anything about consent or healthy relationship skills in standard education. One young man stated, "I've been told I need them. I have not been taught them. I've had a sex-ed class that dealt with anatomy. I have not learned consent or healthy relationship skills." (Source: harvard.edu.)

These studies show that parents are unwilling or feel unprepared to have these conversations, so they avoid them. If your program is at the level you want it to be, Coach, and you call it a "family" all the time, and you call it a "brotherhood" all the time, and you call the key to coaching "relationship building" (which I would agree with), but you are unwilling to talk about things like sexual health, safe-sex practices, consent, and relationship skills, you cannot claim you have a "family."

This is especially true, knowing that players are desperate for this information and you, as a trusted adult, are a potential source for it. What's more, Coach, we know that if you don't fill this void in the vacuum of information, they will turn to other places for it, and the other places they will turn are the Andrew Tates, the incels, and the misogynists of the manosphere. Pornography will become their go-to "university" on what sex actually is, and angry sexists will tell them that what's causing them angst is women. If you don't do this work, these other voices will, and the other voices will teach your players to stay in #TheManBox, to blame others, to dominate others, and to not have real relationships or emotional fluency (Source: theatlantic.com). So, we have to move past saying, "They don't want this for me." As a matter of fact, they do want it, and they need it.

The fourth pain point I hear is various versions of, "Kip, I can't change who they are. That's what their parents are for," or "I can't change 19 years of bad parenting." I would argue that you don't settle for that defeatist mindset when it comes to teaching them skills on the football field, the basketball court, or the tennis court. You don't settle for, "Well, their parents or their previous coaches have already built who they are as a player, and I'm just kind of stuck with it." You don't believe that because you do nothing but player development. You do nothing but skill development in your work, and you go about trying to help your players unlearn and offload bad habits and then try to build them into something better. I've heard coach after coach give recruiting pitches (and I used a version myself) along the lines of, "Hey, you know what? We're getting the raw materials, and we're going to find the diamond out of the coal." We can do the same thing when it comes to who our players are as people.

Also, I don't know if bad parenting is the only cause of poor behavior. Often, parents are doing their best, but the players are being socialized into #TheManBox without them knowing. I don't know why we settle for this excuse. If you really believed that you were unable to overcome bad parenting, you wouldn't have any expectations, rules, or standards of any kind up on your walls. If you thought parents made some players untrainable, then you wouldn't bother with them in the first place. You'd just tell your administration, "Whatever happens with our guys off the court happens." But you don't do that (and they wouldn't accept that stance). You try to demand obedience and force change. The truth is, you can help players unlearn the programming and escape #TheManBox no matter what their upbringing was.

Finally, I get told various versions of, "Kip, if we commit time to this framework and all of what you're asking me to do with #MirrorTraining, it will detract from our ability to win." My first question is, how? What aspect of having better people in the locker room who are always available to play (because you don't have any suspensions from poor behavior choices) is a detriment to winning? Take it further and ask yourself, why are people who are always available and now more capable of reading and reacting to each other's emotional states accurately going to lose? What part of that formula equals a worse chance to win? Better people, always available, reading and flowing with each other through all the angst of a game without losing their minds in moments of anger or non-values-aligned behavior—that recipe equals losing? It doesn't.

What people are actually saying indirectly when they ask this is, "Kip, your record as a coach was bad, and I think it was because you did #TeamsOfMen instead of more shell drills." Yes, my record as a coach is not what I would have dreamt for myself when I took the job. But it doesn't mean that YOU can't win using this framework. What if my record as a coach is entirely rooted in my shortcomings as a tactician? What if you are a better tactician and schemer than me? Add your better ability on the whiteboard with the thing I was good at (creating #MirrorTraining opportunities regularly for players in this framework), and I guarantee you that you will have a better record than me. The sky's the limit.

Not to mention, coaches typically cannot point to me how the 15 to 20 minutes I'm asking for bi-weekly for #MirrorTraining would be better spent somewhere else. They can't answer that question because the idea that coaching for better humanity equals coaching for losing is a straw man and a false equivalency.

Reader #MirrorTraining Challenge (Chapter 5): I want you to think back to an aspect of your team's performance about which you said, "We aren't good enough here right now." At the end of the season, no matter your sport, you most likely didn't win the championship. Even if you did, you probably told yourself, "For us to be more successful next year, we need to be better at this."

Now, think about all the ways you moved heaven and earth to develop that aspect of your team's performance. List all the people, books, videos, clinics, texts, emails, and phone calls you made to learn and grow in that area. Recognize from that list that you do know how to upgrade your knowledge in areas you want to. You know how to create a roadmap to developing your skills as a coach to help your players in an area they're lacking.

All you have to do is decide you want to deploy that same eagerness to learn how to help your men blow up #TheManBox. By doing so, you've answered one of the pain points we just talked about. You might not know enough, but you know how to learn more. You've deployed that skill already. You just have to choose to deploy it along this line as well.

CHAPTER 6

A Focal Point for All Ages

A common concern I hear from coaches after one of my presentations or workshops is, "Kip, I really like that message, but I'm a little worried about using words like 'gender,' 'gender violence,' 'misogyny,' 'rape,' and 'sexual assault' because my players are not mature enough. And I'm *really* worried that our players' parents are not going to want us to talk about these types of things."

I completely understand this worry. But I always reply, "While I want to validate your worries, I also want you to know that the work can begin with a universally agreed-upon topic, one that probably has even deeper implications with younger groups like middle schoolers or high school underclassmen." This topic is emotions, or, more specifically, teaching male athletes what emotional intelligence is and how to use it.

Very few parents have ever expressed to us that they don't think their young man could use work to deal with his emotions. Very few parents have ever told us the young man in their house didn't seem like a ticking time bomb from time to time, depending upon the mood they encountered them in. When we talk about "emotional control," we get a lot of head nodding and comments like, "Please, feel free to try and get that built into his toolbelt." In all honesty, when young men are not trained in emotional fluency and agility, their emotions too often spill out, and the resulting behaviors land squarely on everyone in their immediate circle (usually their teammates on the field, their classmates in the hallways, and their family at home). While this work carries weight with our older partners, it has been an immediately impactful launch point in our younger groups as well.

Just this past fall, in a 10-day span, I worked with a Power Five college basketball team, followed by a high school program and then a middle school football team. To be honest with you, despite having fantastic experiences with all these groups, I left thinking that the impact of this work in the middle school environment was ten times that of the other two. Not that it wasn't a positive and inspiring experience for high school and college students, but the middle school kids were sponges. When we got middle school kids' attention (which is a little harder to do with that age group, obviously) when we got them focused on the subject matter, they absorbed the information and tried out the skill sets almost immediately.

The brains of middle school kids are still, as organizational psychologist Adam Grant says, "excited to be operating in scientific mode." They are still open to new ideas. They still embrace curiosity naturally (Source: GreaterGood). Being curious hasn't been policed out of them yet, and they're also quick to deploy whatever it is they are learning at the moment.

Case in point, in a follow-up text later that day, their coach said, "Unreal. A couple of those things you asked the kids to do in naming emotions, I heard them at practice today, which is insane, right?" That's a shocking and awesome development, but it confirmed to me that the work can be done and probably should be started at the middle school level, as it's a perfect storm for harm caused by a lack of emotional intelligence, fluency, and agility. But it's also the perfect storm for kids to get awesome reps at a young age and start to define themselves in positivity and values-aligned behavior. It's always easier to be proactive than reactive.

Here's how we start emotional intelligence, fluency, and agility conversations with all of our age groups. We either bring a bottle of water (with the labels torn off) or we ask one of the athletes to bring up their backpack. (For whatever reason, in the 21st century, very few schools are using lockers anymore. I know my kids go to school with two or three backpacks attached to their bodies at all times and never stop at their locker.) We then ask the players in the audience, "Hey, take a look at your teammate Johnny's backpack. How much do you think it weighs?" or "Take a look at this water bottle. It's about three-quarters full, and Coach Kip has torn the label off. How much do you think it weighs?" Then we give them time to shout out answers, and we'll either write them on the whiteboard or put them on the screen if we have a projector set up.

The students will yell out their answers: "Oh, it's four pounds," "It's 12 pounds," or "it's 16 fluid ounces." We'll get a sea of guesses, which is fine. The point is to engage them (especially the younger groups) and let him shout things out. They spend all day being told to be quiet, so we let this be two minutes when they can just let it rip!

Once they've given us a ton of answers, we stop the group, bring them back to center, and say, "Hey, we appreciate the answers, but they're all wrong because the current weight in pounds or fluid ounces means nothing. It's entirely dependent upon how long I ask you to carry it. If it's eight pounds today, it'll be a little heavier tomorrow if you never get to set it down. It'll be a little heavier a week from now if you never get to set it down. It'll be really heavy a year from now if you never get to set it down. There will come a point when it is too heavy to carry, and we either drop it onto a desk and move things around in the tussle or, if it's a bottle, we squeeze it and let water burble up through the top and spill out over everything around us."

We then talk about how #TheManBox teaches you at a young age to control, stifle, and ignore emotions. It tells you to bottle them up or "put them in a backpack" and just carry them around without ever addressing them or setting them down throughout your day. We tell the students, "If you can't learn to name these emotions, if you can't learn to define what you're feeling from these emotions, if you can't learn to process these emotions so you can take them out of your backpack (or empty your water bottle in the sink), eventually, you're going to drop it on somebody, or you're going to spill the water on everyone around you."

That visual, especially with younger students, has been powerful, and it's worked to get them thinking, "When I carry this anger around and try to stuff it down, most often, I end up exploding later somewhere due to some trivial thing. Then I feel bad for the people who got in the way of my rage moment, people I wasn't even mad at. I was just carrying these things for so long that I couldn't bear the burden anymore." The entire session takes no more than 10 minutes, and it's been a very successful discussion starter for this framework with a younger audience.

Another framing that we've used (especially at the lower levels) asks the players to lay out the set of rules their coach has given them. Then we say, "Do you think about the coach's rules during school? Do you think about the coach's rules when you're at home? Why do we ask you this? Because we don't want you to only follow the rules because the coach said so. That's called seasonal character. We want you guys to live above and beyond the rules all the time. That's called values-aligned behavior." Once again, this does work at the high school and college levels, but it's been very successful with middle school teams.

We instruct coaches to ask themselves, "Do our guys have the processing skillset to behave the way that we, their teachers, and their parents want them to without the carrot of the season and playing time hanging over them? Are they doing things that way just because they don't want to lose their allowance, or are they doing things that way because they've started to form their own belief systems around right and wrong? If their thinking is simply, 'Due to the carrot this adult is dangling in front of me, I'll abide by the rules, but once it's gone, I'll just go back to living and doing things the way I've always done them,' then what has this player actually learned?"

By unlearning the idea that "emotions are for girls" and learning that men, too, are fully capable of emotional fluency and using emotional agility to make the best choices even when we feel the worst, we shift from a seasonal-character-defined team to a values-aligned-behavior one. As coaches, we go from believing we need to micromanage all behavior to simply witnessing our players' decision-making paradigms. We can sit back and relax, not only as they play how we coached them to but also with the confidence that their decision-making paradigms will take over in a good way in life situations.

We then progress to naming emotions, putting actual titles to the feelings they have because, often, they have never done it. The moment they name an emotion, they take a giant stride toward taming that emotion. I share with them how the phrase "That's *crazy*, Coach" was one of the most used in my time as a head coach. We ask them, "What do you all think *crazy* means?" As they share their answers, we write them down so that everyone can see them. Inevitably, you get a difficult-to-ignore (for both coaches and players) graphic showing how many different meanings everyone uses to describe "crazy." How we use these five letters for everything from "I'm mad" or "I'm frustrated" to "I'm angry" shows how simple our emotional vocabulary can be.

I remember having a sit-down meeting with a captain of mine to let him know he would no longer be a starter. That is never an easy conversation, and I expected him to react negatively to the news. However, as he processed the information, all he could get out was, "That's just crazy, Coach." I told him that many times throughout our relationship (at that point, I had been his coach for over three years), I had heard him say, "That's crazy," to me to describe his feelings when he was visibly excited, angry, or confused. Today, I needed him to use a more accurate term for how he was feeling. I told him he didn't need to do that for me but for himself, that in handling this demotion in status as a player, he needed the best version of himself to name exactly what he was feeling so he could start to deal with it. He could say, "Coach, I'm so let down by this," or "Coach, I feel betrayed by you." Hell, he could say, "Coach, I'm absolutely devastated." Any of those would be more beneficial than settling for saying, "That's crazy," over and over again.

As an expert on the issue of emotional fluency, Dr. Susan David, author of the book *Emotional Agility*, says that naming emotions is the key to better behavior when you're confused by them. When you can define emotions more accurately, you set yourself up for a better chance at identifying how you need to respond to them. We take her work further and implore the young men we work with to put the words "I'm feeling" in front of the emotion they, hopefully, are now able to define. By doing this, they remove the idea that they must be that emotion incarnate. They are not frustrated. They're feeling the effects of frustration. They are not devastated; they are feeling the effects of devastation. When they know that they are separate from the emotion, they have a better chance of being their best selves despite feeling those emotions. This has been one of the exercises we've enjoyed success with while working with middle school kids.

A lot of young boys in middle school are going to be scared to share because, to many of them, it's akin to sharing a character fault. #TheManBox has taught them that anything associated with feelings is unmanly. They're going to worry, "These guys are going to think I'm soft," "These guys are going to think I'm a girl," or "These guys are going to think I'm a pussy." They assign all those horrible things to themselves and each other because, in the past, any expression of vulnerability was weaponized against them. #TheManBox says, "Hey, take any of that guy's feelings, anything that makes him less, and weaponize it so you can dominate him."

So, you've got to set the stage to provide them with courage. This is something I learned from Jen Fry, who does an amazing job with DEI training across the country. She taught me that in these spaces, we don't necessarily want a safe space (which is a common term chased prior to workshops) because safe spaces can be used to tone-police people. Safe spaces can be used to remove the passion of people who are directly affected by these conversations. Safe spaces can be used to silence people. What we do want are spaces where we're willing to be vulnerable, but we demand respect in these spaces. So, we're never going to flee from conflict, but we're going to demand respect at all times.

We'll have some disagreements in these spaces, and we will share things that are hard to talk about. But if we're courageous and demand respect from one another, then we're modeling for the kids how to have crucial conversations in life. We're showing them the answer to the question: "What do we do when someone gives us something that we know that #TheManBox has told us to weaponize and make fun of them with? What does it look like, instead, to embrace the person's vulnerability and meet them with empathy and compassion?"

Reader #MirrorTraining Challenge (Chapter 6): Think back to the times players in your program had an outburst, either with words or actions, that was harmful and shocking to you, your staff, their parents, or their teammates, moments where you said, "I didn't know he had that in him," or "That's not who he normally is. That was out of character for him." I'm not arguing that those statements aren't true, but now that you've read this chapter, ponder what this young man might have been carrying and for how long. What if you had created space earlier in your season to help that young man unpack those things? Could you have avoided this shocking incident, this out-of-character moment for him?

CHAPTER 7

Community Impact

Earlier in the book, we talked about how changing the world one person at a time is too slow and how true change needs to happen one influencer at a time. That truth exists on every school campus, regardless of the level. Whether it's middle school, high school, or college, your athletes have an opportunity to impact their communities directly, both in the athletic department and the greater campus. Eventually, this impact can expand to cities and states as well. To do this, however, we've got to prep and upload communication skills in our "influencers."

Too often, coaches complain, "My guys don't know how to talk. They can't talk to me, my staff, their parents, or each other. They only know how to text." Then why aren't we creating more spaces and opportunities for reps with those communication skills they lack? If you want your team, which is a community, to be better at communication, then why aren't you consistently having #MirrorTraining and #TeamsOfMen framework discussions about things that matter and honing the players' ability to communicate?

We would all agree that if players can communicate in team spaces, they can communicate in athletic departments. If they can do that, then they are probably better able to do it on campus, at home, and with their friends. Unstated expectations are set-ups for failures (whether intentional or not). If we don't open our guys' eyes to what effective communication is, how can we expect them to be good at it? We would NEVER send them out onto the court or field to execute a play without practicing it for hours beforehand. Why do we do the inverse when it comes to their ability to be better people? Add this to the equation: if we haven't done consistent communication work, we probably haven't built up players' awareness of the influence they wield (and the places they hold it). So, we have a recipe for unskilled communicators who are unaware of how and when they can sway an audience. For true community impact, these two things must change, and the #TeamsOfMen model is the path to doing it.

How do I know this? I've personally seen this process take shape. Many moons ago, I played college basketball at the Division III level. Though not an All-American by any means, I was good enough to be the team captain, play in a hundred games, start for two years, etc., but I had no delusions that my career was going anywhere past the college level. I wasn't good enough to play professionally, and I was at peace with that.

But the influence in the community male athletes have (and remember, the *earned* nature of this platform is something American society should certainly examine) hit me squarely in the face during my college career. I remember working at a basketball camp going into my senior year, and my coach at the time had us working with children from 10 to 14 years old. It was a young group, not toddlers by any means, but a younger group of kids. My college teammates (also serving as camp coaches that particular week) and I would work out during the campers' meal breaks (lunch, dinner, etc.). We'd play, and the campers would watch us while they rested after a long session at camp.

I finished the workout one day, and an assistant coach from our program came up to me and said, "Kip, you're not going to believe this, but see that group of kids over there?" He pointed at some 11- or 12-year-old boys. "They just said to me, 'Hey, Coach, that Kip's really good. Is he going to the NBA?'" We both laughed loudly at this. I knew how ludicrous the question was, but to that group of young kids, I had a status on par with *far better* players. I went over and said hello to the kids, and unbeknownst to my 20-year-old self, I could have influenced them to do or think anything!

Fast forward to five, six years ago, when, as head coach, I took my college basketball team to a local elementary school for a reading day. Mind you, in the midst of the season, we were an under-.500 team. We were not winning our conference. We were not ranked in the top 25 in the country. I loved our guys, but we were not having a championship season. Add to this the fact that we were a Division III basketball team. It's a great level, very competitive, but we don't have the natural athleticism that Division I teams do. (One of my favorite recruiting pitches to parents and players was that D3 equals three inches: three inches less in height per position and three inches less in vertical and lateral explosiveness. The skill level is similar, but the athleticism is not.)

We showed up to this elementary school and had maybe two dunkers on our roster of 15 guys. Our plan was for the whole school to gather in the gym for some skill demonstrations from the players while I told the students about the importance of effort and work ethic to achieve anything. After that, the players would go to different classrooms to participate in reading groups with the kids. When the assembly began, the level of excitement and cheering that we got with our two dunkers was crazy, even though no one on our roster was over six foot eight. It was incredible. This surprised me, but it shocked the guys. "Coach," several of them said to me, "that was louder than some of our home games."

That further solidified in my mind that the power of the male athlete platform is huge. When you put on a helmet or lace-up hoop shoes, younger males believe you can do everything they think a star player can do. They think you are NBA-level, and they give you the same reverence as an all-star, and while you know that's not who you are, they don't.

So, by putting players through consistent #MirrorTraining and #TeamsOfMen sessions, we're teaching them to wield their power for a greater good, not as a pro basketball player but as a professional character-development messenger. For college coaches out there, that's a testimony to our beliefs and also a self-reflection #MirrorTraining moment for you. How are we and our staffs preparing guys, and what tools are we giving them for when they stand up on campus, walk through the hallways, sit in the cafeteria, are interviewed by the local newspaper, are on the local news show, or are on social media? How are we preparing them to make a positive impact in those spaces and have a voice?

Another positive impact on the community that I often experienced in my time making #MirrorTraining the core of our program was when I would get emails, texts, and messages and have personal encounters with community members. I'd be sitting in the cafeteria, for example, with my staff, having lunch, or maybe getting ready for a game on the weekend or something, and a professor I'd never met before (except through maybe an email or a grade check where I saw his or her name) would stop by and say, "Hey, are you guys the basketball coaches?" We'd say yes, and they'd say, "I have [insert player name] in class. I'm just really impressed by how he handles himself," or "Hey, I have [insert player name] in class. He's a pleasure to have in class. It's really awesome that I can count on him for participation and attendance." I think that it is proof of a positive impact on the community when professors are excited to have your players in class, when they are showing up to your games to support the young men you have, not because they're necessarily super fans who want to see you hang banners but because they're invested in the kids and the way conduct themselves because of the work you do.

We had requests for our guys to go to department symposiums and present on the topics of healthy manhood and positive masculinity. We had folks from the university asking, "Can your players meet with this rep from the NCAA to discuss the program you do because we're so proud of the impact it has." We'd have local high school coaches ask our players to present "How to Examine Manhood in the 21st Century" to their teams, and then they'd tell us how engaging our guys were with their players.

Often, I wouldn't go to those presentations because I trusted my guys. I knew the work we'd done to prepare them, and I wanted them to stand in their power and not be distracted by me there or having me answer questions for them. They were ready. All of these anecdotes are evidence of the positive impact your guys can have in doing this work on campus.

Finally, let me call out a self-limiting complaint that coaches (including my past self) use to neutralize one of the most vital "communities" that your players can influence. Think to yourself how often you have said (or heard other coaches say), "Kids these days don't know how to talk to each other. They don't know how to communicate. And you know why? It's those damn cell phones!" Too often, I think coaches trip themselves up on this idea. All our communities are connected through cell phones, and it's not worth fighting. I think that ship has sailed. It's not worth moaning about the old days and how we did this or how we had to do that back in our day.

In truth, the best assistant you can have now is your player's cell phone. You can use it to instantly send your players viral videos, stories, and messages faster than you ever could in the past. You can start teaching them how to use the phone to spread positive education, even unlearning, in their communities. Often, the social media networks your players have are far more expensive than yours. This means they can amplify messages faster and to more people than you can.

Their personal "audience" is another space where this work spreads positive influence and messaging. We used to share with our players "*must follow account*" lists on social media at the start of a season (on Instagram, TikTok, YouTube, X, etc.). We'd give them accounts of experts in the field and voices that spoke to positive masculinity, gender violence prevention, consent training, and healthy relationship skills, and we'd make our guys follow them. We didn't buy them books by these authors, but we made them add them to their feeds because, at some point during each day, they'd be scrolling with their thumbs (like all your players do and you do yourself), and we were hoping that if we populated their feed with more positivity, with more actionable #MirrorTraining-type content, they'd be more likely to see it during the day. Then, all they had to do was hit "share" or "like," and suddenly, that message was amplified to their network. We were activating another way for this methodology to impact a community.

"Community" starts with the player-to-player interaction in your team room, expands to player interactions with other teams in the department, extends further to their engagement with other students on campus, and then encompasses the city or town you're in.

One aspect of community that I think is overlooked too often by male coaches (and honestly, I think guy coaches get wrong more often than not) are sports that have a women's counterpart—men's soccer and women's soccer, men's basketball and women's basketball, baseball and softball, men's T&F and women's T&F, etc.—and the dynamic that exists between the different programs sharing the same space.

The positive impact of the work we did on our ability to be a better partner to the women's basketball team was immeasurable. First, we were one of the few teams in our league that, for a decade, was able to travel with our female counterparts. I'm talking about actually engaging and enjoying traveling on the road with the women's team, sharing the same charter bus during conference play. One of the biggest causes of budget crunches is travel costs, and it's a big burden to pay for two buses going to the same location seven hours away on the same day. I know a lot of departments foot that bill despite the cost and basic common sense because they are worried about male player behavior in proximity to female-identifying players. But between me and the women's coach (Peg Swadener, who was a long-time friend of mine and a fantastic coach), we never had an issue. She didn't have angst about our guys sharing space with her women because she saw the intentional work we tried to do to make our men capable of not causing harm with their words, actions, or beliefs.

Now, we still had to talk and have discussions, but it was such an engaging, positive meshing of our programs that it ended up being one basketball program, not separate women's and men's programs. Obviously, we played separate games and had separate schedules, but we existed together seamlessly.

Other coaches would come to us and say, "How do you do this? How do you all share spaces? How do your programs coexist the way they do?" We would then say it starts with the intentional choice to hold space and have convos with the guys to unlearn some of the things that they think they deserve as men versus what the women's team deserves. We help them drop toxic ideas (like that the boys deserve the back of the bus every trip, that the boys should pick the music that plays over the intercom system, or that the boys should be dropped off first for their meal) and embrace this new version of existing together: not one on top, not one more dominant than the other, existing together as equals. This not only directly impacted the relationship we had with our sister team but also modeled what equality should look like going forward for our men.

The final reframing I want to cover is community service versus service learning. I'll share ways that I used to gauge our community service and contrast that with an enlightening, unlearning moment that was thrust upon me, for which I'm very grateful. Prior to this shift, I falsely believed in the need for our program to "do" community service. I believed we needed to have [X] number of reps or show up [X] number of times and that would be effective community service. Examples of this were when we'd have our guys do capstone presentations at high schools or talk at length to campers in the summer.

In addition, we'd have our juniors pick a community give-back event every year. One year, they might pick doing the yard work for the women's and children's shelter and getting a tour of the facilities. Another year, they might focus on Thanksgiving and giving away free and hot meals to needy families throughout the week. Those are just a few examples the guys would pick, all rooted in the great intentions we had as a program to "do" community service.

About a month before I left my previous institution, I met the new assistant dean for civic engagement. During his first presentation to our athletic department, he laid out the shortcomings of one-off community service and the potential impact service learning could bring. After the session, we set up a meeting, where he said to me, "I've heard all these things about this #TeamsOfMen stuff you do. Tell me about its impact on the community. Tell me about what you guys do." I told him how we were showing up for community service, and he said, "Before you and your team went to these places, did you guys do a debrief or an information session together as a group to lay out your reason for going to these places?"

"No," I said, "I don't think so. The players chose the causes, and I'm assuming that they did some version of research, but it's not like they shared it with their teammates."

"Okay," he said, "when you coordinated with the folks who work in the cause every day, at the sites, did you or the players reach out and ask them about the what, why, or how of their day-to-day experience?"

"No," I replied. "The usual flow was an email or phone call to schedule the date, and then we probably met somebody at the front desk, and they either gave us a tour or showed us where to go to do the work."

"You guys probably took some photos and pictures of the day," he said.

"Yeah, and we put them up on our socials," I answered.

Then he asked, "Did you ask for their permission?"

"No," I said. "We didn't do that." At that moment, I realized that what we were doing wasn't a net positive for the people we were supposedly helping. We were doing performative one-offs with little learning or engaging in the actual realities of the people who work at these spots every day, all day, with little to no fanfare.

This conversation continued for 20 to 30 minutes, in which he pointed out that in the aftermath of our supposed good deeds, we hadn't debriefed as a group about the potential impact we'd had that day. We hadn't followed up with anyone at the sites and asked if we had truly helped or not. We didn't even do the seemingly easy task of talking as a team about what it was we'd done that day, what we had noticed while there, how what we had seen had landed with us. Hell, in almost every instance, we didn't make plans to follow up and be of service further down the road, past our one-time "knights in shining armor" visit.

These realizations hit me like a ton of bricks. In previous #MirrorTraining sessions, I had hammered home to our guys that good intentions are never an excuse for negative impact. Well-meaning intentions do not shield you from accountability for poor impact. If we had been going into these places and having a negative impact, despite our intentions, I was blind to it. And I was embarrassed by this.

One year, we took our team to a women's and children's shelter. Now, even though we're not as tall as Division I teams, we still had six-foot-five, six-foot-six, and six-foot-seven guys on the roster. Often, women and children are at these shelters due to the actions of men, specifically gender violence. And here I was, bringing in strong, athletic, imposing men, which could have triggered past traumas for these women and children. Somehow, I never considered that. Going further, what was the impact of us posting our work at these places, where people toil every day in careers of service and don't get any notoriety? Who were we to post our four-hour day as some type of accomplishment? Did we put any of those people in our pictures? Did we champion their cause? No, we didn't.

That was a low moment for me, but at the same time, it was invigorating. I appreciated being rocked out of my comfort zone and onto a new path. We needed to embrace service learning to truly serve the community the way we wanted to.

Go back to the last community service event you did. Did you and your players reflect before you went on why this was the place you were visiting, on the history of the place, or on why they might need more help? Did you reflect after the event with your guys on how the experience landed with them? What emotions did they feel? What did you witness? What did you notice? How does the time spent in community service sit with you? Did you follow up with the community members you worked with on how your team could continue to support them? Did you ask them what impact you and your players had?

Often, we may have thought we did a great job and helped a lot, but they may have different recollections. They may be thankful for your effort but let you know that it fell short or even had an adverse effect on their day-to-day life. To experience truly transformational service learning, the kind that can really impact the greater community, we have to unlearn and adjust.

Reader #MirrorTraining Challenge (Chapter 7): Here's a way you can get feedback on the impact your guys are having in their communities. First, make an appointment with the head coach of all the women's teams in your department. Ask them for a time that's convenient for them, and then ask them and their players (if you can get their permission) to give you answers on what it's like to interact with the guys on your team at the athletic facilities, on campus, in the dorms, in the community, at lunch, and in the cafeteria. Ask them for feedback on who your guys are to the women in your program, and then do the same with professors and teachers. To ensure anonymity and honesty, you can put protections up on the Google Form or Survey Monkey.

Now, if you get positive feedback, you know you're on the right course in terms of character development. Keep doing what you're doing. However, if you get negative feedback, you've got work to do.

We've had partner programs get feedback about the ways their guys manspread (in the hallways, in the cafeteria, or on the bus). They've gotten feedback bemoaning the words and phrases that their guys might be using (catcalling women in the training room, singing along to sexually explicit songs in the gym when both teams are there, etc.). We've heard from coaches who were told that their guys feel the pitch, the field, and the weight room are theirs by right and try to harass women's teams into leaving whenever it is inconvenient for them to share. If you get similar reports, you now have the proof you need to start the work of #TeamsOfMen.

CHAPTER 8

Sustaining Change

I f you've made it this far in the book, you're versed in the why and how of launching our framework, and you've got some examples of how to #MirrorTrain. Now, we want to show you how a long-lasting commitment to this work equates to a wave of sustainable change in our profession as coaches and in the lives of the young men we serve.

To begin, it's helpful to recognize the following "formula" you possess that lends itself to an obligation to do the work into perpetuity. As long as you have a team, this formula will exist, and as long as this formula exists, you have the perfect recipe to create lasting change in the minds of male athletes.

Ask your players where else they have a constant routine. Where else are they "supposed to be" every day when you're in season (and often, with the way off-season training has evolved in sports, it's not a stretch to say where they are "supposed to be" every week throughout the year)? Where else do they get time and space with other men (or other boys when they're younger) whom they like, respect, and love? That's the first part of this unique formula that I believe coaches have to take advantage of, and it begs you to make this a long-lasting, sustained change and framework you use.

Next, where else do they go where they can be led, taught, or influenced by a trusted coach, mentor, or role model? That's input two of this formula.

Finally, for the third part of the formula, where else do they go every single day where they will be challenged and forced to grow and become better versions of themselves?

So, we have a chosen, regularly occurring space with teammates we love, led by a person we trust, and we show up to these spaces fully prepared to be driven to become better versions of ourselves. We cannot waste this prime opportunity on just growth as a basketball, football, or soccer player. Yes, we can grow the athlete, absolutely, but at the very least, we need to carve out some time to activate this formula for the human being as well (I would argue *equal* time).

Full disclosure: I've had a therapist for 16 years. God bless him. I love him. My commitment to therapy was one of the vulnerable aspects of my life that I'd always share with my players. That gave players permission to come to me and ask, "Coach, how do I find a therapist? How do I find a psychologist?" or "Coach, I feel like I could use therapy. You talked about it. You were okay with it, so I want to explore it." Long story short, it was a connecting point for me to share my vulnerability.

But coming back to this point about sustaining change, my therapist tells me regularly, "Kip, to refuel your capacity to be the dad you want to be, the coach you want to be, the business owner you want to be, the speaker you want to be, I need you to spend time with people you love, to spend time in places you enjoy, and to spend time in conversation with people who challenge you." Real talk.

It is damn near impossible when you're 44 years old to find that time monthly, much less daily. It's not doable with the schedule crunches that come when wearing all the hats we do. It's not realistic in terms of where your friend group actually lives, their schedules versus yours, AND whether or not they want anything more than a cold beer and surface-level conversations about the NFL.

Let's be honest: as we get older, not a lot of us even want to be challenged. We often choose "the matrix," so to speak, and want to stay rooted in who we are rather than expand who we can be. So, when these young men are in our programs, from middle school through college, we must capitalize on their still being OPEN to newness. We need to activate this recipe which does not exist anywhere else in the lifespan of male athletes. Embrace the idea that, as a coach, you will leave an impression not only on your players' lives but how they go about trying to imprint young men in their sphere of influence. Male athletes of every age can tell you a coach who had an impact on them.

Players in their adult years can tell you a story, a snippet, or a quote that recounts some version of, "Well, that's how I was coached." These stories lead to how they go about coaching and mentoring young people themselves later in life. I've had countless colleagues tell me, "When I started coaching, I did it the way Coach Jones, Coach Thomas, and Coach Smith coached me. He won this many games/state titles, so why wouldn't I do it the way he did it." There's a perpetuation of the coaching techniques from our past (almost like fossils we unearth and use again). The style and techniques of coaching are passed to us, and then we pass them on to the players. That's the very definition of sustained impact.

Without the #MirrorTraining approach, it's easy to slip into coaching the same way our coaches did in the 60s, 70s, 80s, 90s, and 2000s, etc. But coaching a particular way "because that's the way we've always done it" is never a recipe for growth and change for the better. I would argue that if we don't shift to the #TeamsOfMen #MirrorTraining framework, we're going to repeat #TheManBox lessons that our coaches used. Blowing up and breaking free of #TheManBox requires us to be different from our coaches.

Now, if you're lucky enough to feel like the coach you had in the past was an escapee of #TheManBox and helped you build emotional fluency, resilience, and healthy relationship skills, awesome. Please go forward and use techniques learned from him. But so often, coaches tell me, "I was coached, I was parented, I was taught the old-school way. And the old-school way made me tough. The old-school way meant I was demeaned, cursed at, and dehumanized because of my errors on the floor. I was called a girl, a wimp, and all kinds of names. I didn't like it at the time, but look at me now. I'm a successful dad and husband, and I've got a good career in business. The old tropes of coaching were what I needed to be who I am today."

I disagree, not with your life being successful, but with what you attribute your success to. I ask you to shift the framing and say, "You know what? I've been underselling my resilience. I survived that bullshit coach, that awful teacher, or the harmful, horrible way I was parented, and I found a way to succeed despite the awful methodology I was exposed to. Imagine who my guys can become if I'm a launchpad of a reimagined manhood, of a positive masculinity, rather than a police agent of #TheManbox. I can help them become as resilient as I was but show them better tools and better methodologies and expose them to better ideas than I was. Then they can take that resilience, and the sky's the limit to who they can become."

Remove the echoes of #TheManBox with a different framing. "I am who I am because my coach swore at me and called me a pussy every day." No, you *survived* that coach. You achieved *despite* that coach. Now permit yourself to imagine the possibilities for your players if you don't coach them the way you were. How many of your guys this year, whatever sport you're in, will go on to be tasked with leading a group of young men? They might one day be coaches. They might be dads. They might be teachers. They might be volunteers. They might be mentors. They might be employers supervising groups of men. What skill sets will you have given them in their time with you that they are likely to copy when they lead those individuals? If the sincerest form of flattery is imitation, and you believe that you're having an impact on your guys, they're likely to imitate you.

Let me tell you a story about when I was lucky enough to be able to start breaking out of the "coach how I was coached" cycle early in my career. I played for Gordie James (who won more than three hundred games at Willamette University, including an NAIA national championship in 1993), and I started my coaching career as an assistant coach with him as well. He was a Hall of Fame head coach by the time I started my first year as his graduate assistant (I was getting my master's degree in teaching during that season). The very first practice, he did something more impactful than any play he ever called for me while I was playing. He came up to me before practice and said, "Listen, this is your first day. I want you to start taking notes on everything you don't like about what I do. I don't want you to write down and copy things that I do that you like. This first day, I want you to write down everything you don't like because you're not here to learn how to be me. You're here to figure out who you are as a coach."

That was such a unique and powerful thing for him to do. I've been in coaching now for 20 years, and I promise you it's not the norm. A lot of times, mentor coaches only share what they think their mentee should do because that's the way they did it. And mentees, for fear of losing out on a promotion or damaging the supposed ladder to success they envision, are loath to question any tactic their mentor uses. However, my mentor told me to take a critical lens to him from day one. I was so fortunate to have that because it gave me an inquisitive mindset from the start.

I'm proud to have passed that forward to my staff. I've been lucky to have hired and worked with so many fantastic coaches, whom I like to think I have given the same freedom and voice to question and challenge me. Many run their own versions of #MirrorTraining and #TeamsOfMen with their programs today, and I hope they are doing it in different and better ways than they observed me doing.

Now, let's discuss how to sustain best practices in lesson plans and activities. Let's talk about how you can make this something you can call your own and keep it living, breathing, and growing.

Number one, focus on introducing players to your program and selling it as unique and something to look forward to. If you're a high school coach, write parent-notification letters and host parent nights explaining the awesome outcomes, potential, and unique settings with, "Look what we're going to expose your son to. Look at the time and the intentional space we're going to give your son to grow as a person and how unique that is going to be for him." Set the expectation that this is the norm for your program.

If you're a college coach, recruit with it. Embed it in your recruiting campaign to players, coaches, and parents that one of the unique factors of the program is the #TeamsOfMen #MirrorTraining framework. "Mom, here are the reasons we do it. Dad, here is the belief we have in the human being you're sending us and whom we're going to send out into the world. We're united in this together." I promise you, because I experienced it for almost ten years, that with that message, you will stand out from everyone else.

Everyone has a highlight film in college recruiting. Everyone has scored touchdowns or hit a bunch of home runs. Those highlight films might have a different graphic. They might have a different filter. They might have a different soundtrack. But everyone shows recruits a version of them. However, very few places will have the tangible, real effects of the #TeamsOfMen #MirrorTraining that your program has. That distinction alone can be what matters in the recruiting game.

Also, when onboarding kids, the players might ask, "Can I expect to see all these promises when and if I commit there?" Recruiting with a #TeamsOfMen framework allows you to fulfill some of your recruiting promises sooner rather than later. You're going to have a hard time quickly fulfilling their expectations of playing time, glory, and accolades, but you can fulfill your promise to do this work immediately.

To keep it growing, tier your #MirrorTraining calendar by class. So, in year one, expose everyone to your plan, your system, and your curriculum. But in year two, you're going to do what you did last year *only* for the newcomers to the program (sixth graders, ninth graders, or freshmen in college). They're going to get exposed to that year-one curriculum. But now you need to figure the how and what of the plan you are using in year two for returners. What are the growth areas? What are the new readings, the new speakers, and the new convo prompts? The quickest way to lose players is to expose them to old, repeated plans. You need a calendar, a progression that allows you to stay fresh, to stay new, to keep them engaged. So, you build out year two, and now you've got a two-prong program.

In year three, your new players are going to do the year-one plan, while the kids who finished that plan last year are going to graduate to the year-two plan. Now you're tasked with building the year-three experience. If you stay true to this process, eventually, you're going to have a four-year program where you know what first-years are doing, second-years are doing, third-years are doing, and fourth-years are doing.

A kid sitting down for the first #MirrorTraining of his junior year doesn't want to feel talked down to. You don't want to hear them say, "Coach, I already know this. You already told me this. I already did this activity, did that game, and did that exercise. What's new? What's in it for me?" So, use one of the best tactics to get kids excited (and battle wandering): novelty (seeing something new, fresh, and out of the norm). It's vital to sustain your players' engagement by keeping the material fresh, and a four-year progression satisfies that.

Next, empower your assistants. In year one, you're going to be the driving force of a lot of this. The calendar, the materials, and the actual who/what/where of what we are doing flow from you as the head coach. You're steering the boat, so to speak. But in year two, year three, and year four, ask your assistants, "Which one of these topics do you want? Which one of these do you feel really comfortable with? What topic are you passionate about?" That allows them to be new voices (remember the power of novelty). It allows them to feel empowered. And it allows your players to see that the assistants matter to the team.

One of the best things I've ever done was something I did after spending probably four or five years running most of the sessions myself. I had a lead assistant who was a phenomenal coach (Coach Chris Horton, the current Head Men's Basketball Coach at Warren Wilson College in North Carolina). I knew his potential and that he was well versed in the #TeamsOfMen training. He'd been there with me and was ready to lead his own sessions. I asked him to take the next step and create sessions specifically designed for our juniors and seniors in the program. He embraced the assignment and created what he called our MEP program (mental resilience, emotional fluency, and positivity). He said, "Kip, I want to tackle those three topics with the juniors and seniors. I think they are a natural progression once you're versed in seeing and escaping #TheManbox."

From that point on, when I had the frosh and sophomores in early unlearning sessions, he led the third and fourth years in the training he had created. When he moved on to another school and his own head coaching job, not only did he have reps in building a calendar and running a program himself, but I had a new curriculum that I'd never done that I could be excited about running or passing on to the next assistant. Empowering your assistants to add their value, voice, and what they're really passionate about makes sustaining the work more possible (and helps you avoid burnout yourself).

You can find sustainability in your commitment to #FeedTheFeedback. Create exit surveys for your players, for every class after every year, and especially for your seniors who are graduating. Ask them for the best parts of what you did in the #TeamsOfMen #MirrorTraining segments. Ask them for things that they felt that they still needed to work on. Ask them for things you felt you could have addressed more or forgot to address at all in their four years in the program. Where did they feel you could use some more work? Ask them if they'd be willing to come back as graduates when they are full adults out in the real world to talk to players about the impact of #TeamsOfMen and how it shows up daily in their lives.

All those points of data and feedback are conducive to allowing more voices and more ownership of your program into the fold. It also relieves some of the stress and the work from your plate, which we all know, as coaches, is a real issue (we probably need to do an entire book on our controlling nature as coaches and ways to unlearn needing that tight grip).

Reader #MirrorTraining Challenge (Chapter 8): Send out a text request to your players saying, *"Guys, give me a few of the phrases or the most common things I say the most during practice and games. When you guys are making fun of me behind the scenes, what are the funny phrases that I say that you imitate?"* If you're worried about your guys giving you the truth, use an anonymous online form, like Google Forms or Poll Everywhere, so they feel safe giving you the true answers.

After you've given them a couple of days to give you feedback, take all their answers and lay them out. Go over what is shared. What are the phrases? What are the words they are hearing the most from you, and are you happy with what they've reported? Are you happy with your soundtrack as a coach? Do you see in their submissions echoes of the things your parents and former coaches and teachers said that used to drive you nuts as a player? Are you using phrases that you do like, that you feel good about, that you want to continue using? Is it good or bad feedback on how you sound to your players? Ask yourself, which one of these do I want to eliminate, and which one of these do I want to keep? How can I grow in my communication? That will allow you to avoid the pitfalls of coaching the way you were coached.

CONCLUSION

Looking Ahead

You've probably heard this axiom many times. Someone, somewhere, before you started coaching, said, "Every coach takes his job knowing he's going to get fired at some point." We know this and accept it as an unavoidable part of our profession. Whether we're coaching middle school kids or Power Five college athletes in football, basketball, baseball, or whatever, we will not be the last coach that the program ever has. We know that at some point, the job is going to end with us being removed. It's just the way of the world. Very few of us get to retire or step away on our own terms. It's usually done for us. We all accept that reality. We all talk about that reality. We all laugh and joke and admit that this is the nature of the beast.

But then, for whatever reason, years later, when we're caught up in the job itself, we forget that we accepted that premise from the beginning. We start making our coaching decisions based on not wanting to lose our job (because of fear, pride, or a combination of both), but we knew that it was an inevitability when we signed up.

When we are in that mindset, when we have tunnel vision directed solely by "I gotta make these decisions based on wins and losses... I gotta make these decisions that supposedly will change that scoreboard so I don't get fired," more often than not, we pivot back to the curriculum and coaching styles this book argues against. We decide to win at all costs, and we forget our core values. We stop acting with values-aligned behavior. We forget why we started coaching in the first place. Eventually, we are unable to carry our emotional backpack (the one we talked about in Chapter 6).

All that stress, that anger, that angst over wins and losses becomes untenable, and we explode. And when we explode, the people most likely in the orbit of that explosion and exposed to harm are our loved ones. We might be embarrassed enough by the harm we caused to reflect and resolve to be better. But without adopting what we've discussed in this book (making consistent, intentional space for our guys to blow up #TheManBox, embrace emotional fluency, develop healthy relationship skills, and stand in their power as agents of change), we will simply fall victims to this cycle again.

You're giving yourself a better chance at remaining true to who you want to be as a person, who you want to be as a man, and who you want to be as a coach when you commit your program to #MirrorTraining as the norm, to #TeamsOfMen as the way. You start modeling values-aligned behavior, no matter the results of the scoreboard every night. And your players, because they love you, because they trust you, because they respect you, will follow your lead.

Remember, this does not mean that in the course of your job and before that inevitable end of the journey when you are fired, you shouldn't be competitive. This does not mean that you shouldn't strive to challenge your guys to be better players. You're just adding an impetus to be better human beings. You have a far better chance of getting players to grow on the court if you focus on them off the court as well. They can only grow if you do the work and create the time to help them break free from the constraints of #TheManBox, to help them name their emotions so they can tame them, to help them unlearn ideas about what relationships are supposed to be, to help them onboard consent skills, and to help them recognize and embrace the role they play as influencers in shaping the world for the better.

When I was let go as a coach, a lot of my colleagues and coaches that I competed against for years on the scoreboard reached out to me, and none of them said, "Kip, I'm really going to miss prepping for your press," or "Kip, I really respected your matchup zone defense," or "Kip, we really had a hard time guarding that floppy off a pin-down." Nobody brought tactics and schemes up. Instead, they said, "You know what, at the end of the day, the way you treated your young men, the way you tried to grow your young men, is why I respect you," and "Kip, everybody knows the work you put in to build men of quality. Damn, I respect it." That's the type of respect you want to strive for. That's the type of observation of your true intent that fuels your inner values. It's not your win-loss record. It's not what was on the scoreboard before you were let go. It's the work and embracing this framework that will fuel and reinforce you as a man.

One last thing I want you to do before you're finished with this book is a final #MirrorTraining exercise that I think will lead you to a further relationship with us at #TeamsOfMen. Make a list—on paper, Google Sheets, Microsoft Excel, wherever you keep lists—of your expenditures as a coach and label it "Professional Development." If you're relatively new to the profession, include the expenditures from the past year. If you've been a coach for longer, examine the last three years or maybe even the last five years. Label them by category: "Hey, this was where we went for a better plan on offense. This is where we went for weight training guidance. This is where we went for nutrition. This is how much we spent on that defensive scheme analysis." What was your total expenditure on professional development?

Now repeat that same exercise, but this time write down expenditures related to anything that addressed what we talked about with #TeamsOfMen and #MirrorTraining in this book. Compare the two numbers. How do you feel about the comparison of expenditures? We all believe (and probably have demanded of our players) the importance of "putting your money where your mouth is." If you talk to your players consistently about how to be good human beings and how to grow in respect and character, awesome. But what money choices have you made to help you accomplish those lofty goals?

I suggest that the first thing you do after putting this book down is join our membership model, which will give you access to conversation prompts, discussion ideas, current curriculum, videos, shares, and lesson plans, all delivered monthly to you. And it will give you a significant discount on workshops from us in person with your guys. That's the next launch, the next step with #TeamsOfMen.

If you're thinking, "Well, Kip, that's a pretty obvious money grab from you," you're damn right it is. We never question the "money grab" of basketballs, football pads, or baseball gloves. We never hesitate to swipe our credit cards (a recent study by *Forbes* estimated Power Five schools dole out over six figures in expenditures per athlete). But the moment someone (like me) charges for products and services in the realm of actual character development, we hesitate or clutch pearls. Don't. I would never argue that your players are not worth the money you spend on their athletic development. Of course, they are. I'm simply telling you their future humanity is also worth your investment (both in time and money).

Looking forward to seeing you on the path!

THANK YOU FOR READING MY BOOK!

DOWNLOAD YOUR FREE GIFTS

Just to say thanks for buying and reading my book, I would like to give you a few free bonus gifts, no strings attached!

Scan the QR Code:

#MirrorTraining

I appreciate your interest in my book, and value your feedback as it helps me improve future versions of this book. I would appreciate it if you could leave your invaluable review on Amazon.com with your feedback. Thank you!

www.ingramcontent.com/pod-product-compliance
Lightning Source LLC
Chambersburg PA
CBHW062102270326
41931CB00013B/3184

* 9 781963 793727 *